Earn a Debt-Free College Degree!

No Scholarship? No Problem.

CYRUS VANOVER, MBA

Copyright © 2013 Cyrus Vanover

No part of this book may be reproduced or transmitted in any form whatsoever, either electronic or mechanical, including photocopying, recording, or by any informational storage or retrieval system without the express written, dated, and signed permission of the author.

The information presented herein represents the views and knowledge of the author as of the date of publication. This book is for informational purposes only. The author does not accept any responsibility for any liabilities resulting from the use of this information. While every attempt has been made to verify the information provided, the author cannot assume any responsibility for errors, inaccuracies, or omissions.

Things Change

All of the information in the examples in this book is current as of the date of publication (prices, policies on exam credits, etc.). However, the one thing you can count on in the world of higher education is that things are always in a constant state of change. Schools may change their policies on the number of challenge exam credits they accept, the total number of credits needed to graduate, and many other things. And of course, you can always count on tuition to go up, up, up. Rarely does it ever go down.

If you discover that a price or policy from a particular school is different from what is quoted in this book…guess what? It changed. Nevertheless, by following the examples given in this book, you should be able to map out your own degree program through the school of your choice and still be able to earn a college degree for very little money.

CONTENTS

Introduction 1
1. Understanding the Ivory Tower 5
2. Low-Hanging Fruit 21
3. Hard Work University 39
4. Tuition-Free Is the Way to Be 51
5. The United States Service Academies 59
6. Challenge It! 77
7. Do You Accept the Challenge? 93
8. Ace It! 105
9. Big Savings on the Road Less Traveled 121
10. The Assessment Schools 133
11. Join the Military for a Free College Degree 153
12. Affordable College Courses 175
13. Some Assembly Required 193
14. Looking Back 221

INTRODUCTION

During that magical time in history when glam rock was topping the charts, the Apple II ruled the personal computer market, and the Cold War was nearing its end, I was quickly approaching high school graduation. Like most of my classmates, I was gazing hard at life's crystal ball to see which path I should take. Would it be college, a job, or perhaps the military?

The town I grew up in was really nothing more than a small coal mining community deep within the Appalachian Mountains of Virginia, not far from the Kentucky border. It had a total population of around 1,500, including a movie theater that only showed one movie at a time (when the projector was working), a diner that was stuck in time in 1940's decor, no traffic lights, and no four lane roads. It was like Mayberry…with coal mines. A land of opportunity it was not.

The two main industries that employed people in the community were coal mining and healthcare. The career options were limited to either working in the coal mines or working in healthcare taking care of all the people who got sick from a lifetime of working in the coal mines. That was about it. With such limited career options available, I knew I would have to figure something out fast if I wanted to pursue a different path. But what would that path look like?

The general consensus among those who were older and wiser who offered advice (whether it was requested or not) was that college was the way to go. "Stay in school" was something I heard frequently. From time to time I heard the occasional variation of the theme such as "don't drop out" or "go to school and make something of yourself," but the underlying message was always the same.

The military option also had potential. Unfortunately, I just didn't know enough about it to make an informed decision. The only real concept of military life I had was from the movies. I would think of such movies as *Full Metal Jacket* or *Apocalypse Now* and have second thoughts. Perhaps movies about the Vietnam War weren't the best examples of modern military life, but it was all I had to work with. This left earning a college degree and starting a new life in a new place as the only option that made sense. But didn't that cost a lot of money? Wouldn't I have to take out a huge loan to finance a college education? How were others able to make it happen? There was only one thing that could explain how so many were able to do it: They were in debt up to their eyeballs.

The whole college loan thing perplexed me. As best as I could tell, it was a Catch-22. Yes, with a college degree I could earn more than someone who didn't have a degree. However, after earning a degree and starting a career, I would then have to use my stronger earnings potential to repay the student loans that enabled me to earn more in the first place. Is your head spinning yet? Mine was. I struggled to see the logic.

There had to be a better way; I just knew it. Could a person earn a college degree without accumulating a mountain of debt that would result in years of servitude to the lender? Was there such a thing as an affordable college degree that would enable a student to graduate without owing many thousands of dollars? With these questions in mind I started to do a little research to see just what was out there. No stone was left unturned. What I found was truly surprising and by implementing several of the strategies I discovered, I was able to earn my degree and graduate completely debt-free.

The chapters that follow reveal the strategies I discovered. And no, they have nothing to do with scholarships. There are plenty of books on scholarships available, if that's what you're looking for. These are strategies anyone can use to save a bundle of money. You don't have to be the valedictorian of your high school class to make them work, either. You can use one or two of these strategies to save a few thousand dollars or you can combine several of them to really deal a knockout blow to the tuition monster and graduate completely debt-free.

CHAPTER 1

Understanding the Ivory Tower

"I could have been a Rhodes Scholar...except for my grades."

– Duffy Daugherty

They're out to get your money. From the largest corporations all the way down to the fruit and vegetable stands beside the road, businesses of all sizes are competing for your cash. Billions are spent each year in advertising to attract your attention and convince you that your life will be a miserable mess unless you buy their products or services. We've grown accustomed to a constant bombardment of advertising and tune much of it out as we go about our daily activities. As savvy shoppers we compare prices and brands, clip coupons, read product reviews, and generally do a good job of protecting our financial assets.

There is, however, one sector of the economy that does very little advertising and even turns many people away, yet people are practically beating down the doors to get in to give them money. Parents often save for years just so their children can spend money at these places. And it's considered normal to take out enormous loans to the tune of tens of thousands of dollars to turn over to these places. We're talking, of course, about colleges and universities.

It has become an accepted standard in society that if you want to do well in life, you need to earn a college degree. And who doesn't want to do well in life? Young children are often told they must improve their grades so they can be accepted into college. The alternative, they are told, is a hard life. Sadly, it's not poor childhood grades that keep many people from earning a college degree; it's the cost. College tuition is increasing at a rate that is substantially more than the rate of inflation. It's even increasing faster than the cost of medical care. Economists call it an "education bubble," while others call it nuts.

Why Is Tuition So Expensive?

So, why on earth is tuition so expensive these days? What great expenses do colleges and universities have that requires them to charge so much? The main reason why colleges and universities charge so much is because, well, they can. If you had a product or service that people were lining up and down the street for, would you charge a premium for it? I would. Colleges and universities are no different. They have what people want and most have no qualms about charging as much as they can get away with. This is the reason why schools that are sitting on endowments worth billions (such as the Ivy League schools) still charge outrageous tuition – because they can.

Another reason why college tuition is so expensive is because schools have a bad habit with extravagant spending. And old habits die hard. Schools spend big bucks on fancy buildings with immaculate landscaping. Most schools also have several sports teams that require expensive facilities and fields. The larger schools have epic-size sports stadiums that cost millions of dollars with annual operating budgets larger than many small towns. The head coaches of these great sports teams are paid millions each year. Their salaries are often many times more than the schools' presidents. While it's always nice to have great school sports teams to root for, they come at a heavy price that is often neatly bundled in with your tuition.

Expensive sports teams are not the only thing schools are spending big bucks on. Increasingly, there is an expectation for schools to provide more and more amenities to attract students such as posh living quarters, a variety of on-campus dining experiences, leisure facilities, high-end exercise facilities, and the list goes on and on. Today's college campuses have more in common with Club Med than the education-focused centers of higher learning they were just a few short decades ago.

And finally, some economists believe part of the problem lies with student loans themselves, specifically, the ease of qualifying for these loans. With so much "easy money" available, schools can raise prices as high as they want and people will still be able to come up with the cash to pay for their tuition and other expenses.

In short, the "higher education bubble," as some are calling the rapid rise in tuition prices, is the culmination of several factors including a high demand for the product, extravagant spending on facilities and amenities, and the ease of qualifying for student loans. It is a perfect storm of circumstances that has converged to swiftly drive up costs while pushing students deeper into debt.

Do You Really Need a College Degree?

Before you decide to jump into a college degree program you should take some time to consider whether you really need a college degree in the first place. What are your goals in life? Are you perhaps confusing a desire for a college degree with a need for one? They aren't the same thing. If you desire a college degree, why? Are you interested in earning a college degree because it's expected of you or because all of your friends are doing it? Or is a college degree a vital component of a long-term career plan you have carefully considered and mapped out?

These are not questions to be taken lightly. It's truly shocking how many students go through two, three, or more years of college before even declaring a major and figuring out what direction in life they want to go. There are, of course, those who argue that this is a critical time in a person's life when a student "finds" herself. Throughout the ages many academics, theologians, and philosophers have come up with a technical term to describe such a situation—baloney.

For each year a student spends "finding" herself, she is racking up many thousands of dollars in student loan debt. This debt *must* be repaid. The monthly student loan payments start shortly after graduation and don't end until the debt is paid *in full*. Students can't even shake the student loan monkey off their backs by declaring bankruptcy. Even if you declare bankruptcy, you are still required to pay off all student loans *in full*.

There are many ways to "find" yourself that don't require taking out student loans. You can work full-time for awhile, join the military, join the Peace Corps, or volunteer with a community organization. There are many great opportunities you can explore to expand your horizons that won't leave you drowning in debt.

But, Won't I Miss Out On an Education?

What about the whole "getting an education" thing? Won't you miss out on learning new things if you forgo college? It depends. There are many students who go to college with a serious mindset and determination to study hard and do well. They attend all their classes, do all their assignments to the best of their abilities, and generally know what direction they are going in life. Then there are those students who are just going to school for the social life. They attend all the parties, consume oceans of alcohol, and only show up for classes to take exams. Just because a person attends college doesn't necessarily mean any real learning is taking place. College is what you make of it.

You probably didn't expect to pick up a book on earning a debt-free degree and read something that asks you to think about whether you even need a college degree before enrolling in a program. Far too few stop to think about it before jumping in. This is an enormous mistake that can have lifelong consequences.

Choose Your Major Well

You may have heard the often-repeated statistic that says college graduates earn a higher annual salary than non-graduates. For the most part this is true, but it's really not the end of the story.

While there are certainly many great-paying careers that require a specific college degree, many people who pursue a course of study in a subject that isn't highly marketable often end up in careers that don't require a college degree at all. It happens all the time. If you are certain that college is in your future, be sure you do your homework to see what career options are available for your chosen major after graduation. If you are unable to see a clearly-defined career path for the major you are interested in, it may be a good idea to consider another course of study.

A reality of the job market that isn't often discussed is that there are many high-paying careers that don't require a college degree at all. And on the other side of the coin, there are some college majors that don't lead to much of anything in the job market. Which college majors lead to high-paying careers? Some of the most financially rewarding are the STEM majors (Science, Technology, Engineering, Mathematics). Fewer people pursue these majors because they are often perceived as being more difficult than others, thus increasing the demand for those who graduate with degrees in these fields. Those who have degrees in the STEM majors typically have stronger chances of landing high-paying jobs very quickly after graduating as compared to those who pursued other majors. Just something to think about.

Just about anything in the healthcare field, such as nursing, radiology, physical therapy, respiratory therapy, and others is always a good choice, too. Nursing is perhaps one of the best majors of all time. There are few careers where the unemployment rate is always very low like it is with nursing, even during times of recession. Nurses are always in big demand. A newly graduated registered nurse with an associate's degree can earn far more from day one than most new graduates with bachelor's degrees in other majors. Yeah, it's *that* good. Nursing is also a very diverse field. Nurses can work in many different areas including the ER, ICU, surgery, pediatrics, home health, nursing administration, nursing education, and others. Nurses can even continue their education and earn six-figure salaries as nurse practitioners, midwives, or nurse anesthesiologists.

Great Pay – No Degree Required

There are many great career opportunities that don't require a college degree at all. As you can see in the following list, some of these pay very well. This is just a small sample of the many opportunities that are out there to give you a little extra to think about before enrolling in a college degree program. Some of these jobs can be learned through on-the-job training, while others, such as air traffic control, require the completion of a formal training program (but no college degree). Many people who become air traffic controllers, for example, receive their training (for free) while serving in the military.

Career	Average Annual Salary
Air Traffic Controller	$126,000
Real Estate Broker	80,000
Criminal Investigator	69,000
Manufacturing Sales Representative	51,000
Plumber	49,000
Locomotive Engineer	63,000
Nuclear Power Reactor Operator	73,000
Elevator Installer and Repairer	69,000
Recording Studio Sound Engineer	47,000
Funeral Director	52,000

Make Sure Your School Is Accredited

What is it that makes a college or university legit? Is it a campus with big, beautiful buildings? Or perhaps a great sports team? How about a really nice library? Surely that counts, right? The one thing that makes a college or university legit is its accreditation.[1] If you attend a school that is not properly accredited, you are at risk of either earning a college degree you can't use or earning college credits that can't be transferred. Either way, you will lose out on a lot of money and all the effort you put into completing your courses.

Why would anyone attend an unaccredited school? Sadly, few people bother to check the status of a school's accreditation. They often look at the nice buildings and other facilities and simply assume everything's fine in the accreditation department. This isn't always the case. Schools are occasionally put on academic probation by their accrediting agencies, which should be a big red flag for prospective students. And from time to time a school performs so poorly that its accreditation is revoked. It happens more often than most people realize. In many states schools can continue operating without any accreditation and many students may be unaware that anything is wrong. Don't assume anything. Always look into a school's accreditation before enrolling.

---

[1] There are some exceptions to this. All new schools, for example, must start off without any accreditation. Accreditation is obtained after it is demonstrated that certain standards have been met. There are also some schools that choose to forgo accreditation, like some religious schools. An example of this is Bob Jones University in South Carolina, a highly respected school with excellent academic standards that has not pursued regional accreditation for religious reasons.

Navigating the Accreditation Jungle

Okay, so we've established that checking into a school's accreditation is a good thing. But how do you check it? What exactly should you look for? When you think of a college accrediting agency in the United States, your first thought is probably that of a great, centralized accrediting agency headquartered somewhere in Washington, D.C. It's probably not too far from the Department of Education and is housed in one of the city's many stately-looking office buildings, right? This image couldn't be further from the truth.

In the United States the gold standard of accreditation for colleges and universities is known as regional accreditation. Instead of a large, centralized agency, the job of evaluating and issuing accreditation for colleges and universities has been broken up into six separate agencies. This makes the job much easier since evaluators don't have to travel nearly as far from their home bases to visit and evaluate each school. Each of the six regional accrediting agencies is responsible for making sure all colleges and universities (all that apply for accreditation, anyway) meet minimum standards. Not only do they evaluate colleges and universities, but they also evaluate high schools, middle schools, and elementary schools as well.

In addition to evaluating and issuing accreditation for schools in the United States, the six regional accrediting agencies also do the same for schools that apply from outside the United States. These are typically schools that are interested in attracting students from the United States (for their tuition money, why else?).

Each of the six regional accrediting agencies is considered equivalent to the others. Transferring course credits from a school with east coast accreditation to a school with west coast accreditation, for example, is usually not an issue. There is, of course, nothing that requires a school to accept credits in transfer. Whether or not a particular school accepts transfer credits is entirely up to them. Nevertheless, as long as you earn a "C" or above and the school holds regional accreditation, you should be able to transfer college credit (as long as the courses fit in your degree plan).

The six regional accrediting agencies in the United States and the areas they cover are:

New England Association of Schools and Colleges
www.neasc.org

- Connecticut
- Maine
- Massachusetts
- New Hampshire
- Rhode Island
- Vermont

North Central Association of Colleges and Schools
www.ncacasi.org

- Arizona
- Arkansas
- Colorado
- Illinois
- Indiana
- Iowa
- Kansas
- Michigan
- Minnesota
- Missouri

- Navajo Nation
- Nebraska
- New Mexico
- North Dakota
- Ohio
- Oklahoma
- South Dakota
- West Virginia
- Wisconsin
- Wyoming

Middle States Association of Colleges and Schools
www.msche.org

- Africa
- Europe
- Delaware
- District of Columbia
- Maryland
- New Jersey
- New York
- Pennsylvania
- Puerto Rico
- The Middle East
- US Virgin Islands

Southern Association of Colleges and Schools
www.sacs.org

- Alabama
- Central and South America
- Florida
- Georgia
- Kentucky

- Louisiana
- Mississippi
- North Carolina
- South Carolina
- Tennessee
- Texas
- The Caribbean
- Virginia

Western Association of Schools and Colleges
www.wascweb.org

- California
- East Asia
- Hawaii
- Guam
- American Samoa
- Palau
- Micronesia
- Northern Marianas Islands
- Pacific Rim

Northwestern Association of Schools and Colleges
www.nwccu.org

- Alaska
- Idaho
- Montana
- Nevada
- Oregon
- Utah
- Washington

It's very easy to determine whether the school you're interested in has regional accreditation or if there is any problem with its accreditation status. All you have to do is go to the web site of the regional accrediting agency that oversees schools in the state where your school is located. Each of the six regional accrediting agencies maintains a list of schools it accredits. If your school is accredited, it will be included in this list. In addition, be sure to review the list of schools that are either on probation or have received warnings for deficiencies to make sure your school isn't listed.

Specialized Distance Learning Accreditation (Deeper Into the Rabbit Hole)

Before online learning became common in colleges and universities, there were some schools that offered career certificates in such fields of study as auto mechanics, personal training, legal assisting, interior decorating, and others that could be completed entirely by distance study. Some of these schools even offered high school diplomas and college degrees. Although these correspondence schools didn't quite have what it took to earn regional accreditation, there was still a need for some kind of accrediting agency to validate their programs. The Distance Education Training Council (DETC) was created in 1955 to fulfill this need.

Although DETC accreditation is recognized by the United States Department of Education, there are some limitations to DETC accredited programs you should be aware of. First, you may have trouble transferring any credits earned through a DETC accredited school to a school with regional accreditation. Although there is a handful of schools with regional accreditation that will accept DETC courses in transfer, it's too much of a gamble to risk it. Second, if you do graduate with a degree from a DETC accredited school, you may have some difficulty being admitted into graduate school. Yes, there some schools that will accept DETC degrees, but why take the chance?

There are now so many great options in distance learning through schools with regional accreditation that it no longer makes sense to go with a school that only has DETC accreditation. All of the degree-granting institutions mentioned in this book have regional accreditation; there are no exceptions.

What This Book Is Not

This is not another book on how to get scholarships and grants.

If you browse through your local bookstore for a book on how to lower your tuition bill, you will find some books that claim to show you the way. In fact, there are several of them. The only problem with these books is that most of them focus on scholarships and grants – nearly all of them.

Scholarships and grants are great, if you can get them. These books make it sound like it's very easy to get this money, as though organizations have the money lying around and they're just looking for someone to give it to. The only problem with this is every college student on the planet has read those books and is submitting applications for the same stuff you are. This doesn't mean it's impossible to score some scholarship money, but know up front that it's a numbers game and it takes a lot of work. Expect to spend many hours searching scholarship databases, filling out applications, and writing essays. And then you sit back and wait for the results – and wait, and wait, and wait.

Apply the strategies in this book to your degree plan first. If you do, and you realize you will still owe some money to your school, then by all means, apply for as many scholarships and grants as you possibly can.

Why This Book Is Different

This is the book you should read first. It has nothing to do with scholarships (with the exception of one unique scholarship program). The only grant that is even mentioned (albeit sparingly) is the Pell Grant, and that's only because it is so common. The purpose of this book is to cover the many strategies available that let you earn college credit at cut-rate prices so that you don't even have to consider the possibility of taking out a student loan for any reason. By following the strategies in this book you will be able to choose a school, map out a degree plan, and then earn your degree in such a way that you will owe very little (or nothing) after graduating.

Before We Jump In...

There is a popular saying that says, "if you repeat something often enough, eventually it becomes true." So it is with higher education and the process of earning a college degree. We are conditioned from an early age to think that college is very expensive. To earn a college degree and do well in life, we must take on debt to pay for it so we can land a great job after graduation and live happily ever after.

The reality of student loans is not always so rosy. As this book is being written, the unfortunate news of one student's experience is making headlines: "Alumna Sues College Because She Hasn't Found a Job." This student owes close to six figures in student loans after graduating and the monthly student loan payment still has to be paid, somehow. There is no guarantee that a college degree will lead to a great job. Choose your major carefully and use every means you can to reduce the financial burden before you enroll.

In the chapters that follow we'll take a look at what you can do up front to put an end to the student loan monster. So, grab a glass of your favorite beverage, sit back in a nice, comfy chair, and let your mind be open and receptive to some new ideas on earning affordable college credit and completing your degree for very little money. How little, you may be wondering? Anywhere from free to no more than the price of a good used car. We'll say no more than $15,000 for a bachelor's degree from an accredited school. Impossible? Not at all.

Let's see how it's done…

CHAPTER 2

Low-Hanging Fruit

"Economists report that a college education adds many thousands of dollars to a man's lifetime income – which he then spends sending his son to college."

– Bill Vaughn

Easy Savings

Human nature can be a really interesting thing to observe. Have you ever sat on a bench in a crowded mall or on a busy street and just watched people as they go about their activities? As Yogi Berra once said, "you can see a lot just by looking." One thing that has been a continual source of amusement (and sometimes frustration) to me is the parking lot cruiser. I'm talking about the person who circles a parking lot fifteen times just to get a space that's two spots closer to the store than the one he kept passing by. Why not park at the end of the lot and walk to get some exercise? Why not park at the end of the lot to protect your car from getting dinged up from a runaway shopping cart or from someone parking too close to you and ramming the side of your car with his car door? Why not save a little gas and park *somewhere*, already?

Human nature can also be an interesting thing to observe when it comes to higher education. I am always perplexed when I see people completely bypass affordable schools and go straight for the more expensive ones, especially when they have to take out significant student loans to make it happen. Why skip a perfectly good state university for a much more expensive private school? Why do so many attend expensive out-of-state schools when there are many great schools to choose from in their own states? This is how so many people get in deep financial trouble while earning a college degree. They skip over the easy savings offered by affordable schools in the belief that more prestigious (read…expensive) schools will give them a better chance at succeeding in their future careers. But is there any truth to this?

At this point I could quote a laundry list of research that demonstrates that success in your future career has far less to do with the name of the school on your diploma and far more to do with your own personal ambition, drive, study habits, and old-fashioned go get 'em attitude. But instead of boring you with a list of facts, figures, charts, and graphs, how about we take a look at a practical illustration to make the point?

A Tale of Two Students

Let's consider two students who are each studying to be registered dietitians. They are both majoring in nutrition science and the average salary for this field of work, according to Payscale.com, is $36,000 to $69,000 per year.

The first student, Aaron, took the advice of his high school guidance counselor who told him he should attend the most prestigious university that would accept him to give him the best chance of a successful career. The advice sounded reasonable and he was able to gain admission to

High Society University, a private university in another state. Aaron wasn't worried at all about the high cost of High Society's tuition. After all, this was an *elite* school and he was confident the name of the school on his diploma would give him an edge in the job market.

The second student, Sarah, was concerned about the prospects of going deep in debt to earn her degree and chose to attend a local community college for her first two years of school. She planned on transferring to an affordable state university to finish her degree and graduate.

Fast forward four years. Both Aaron and Sarah graduate, pass their state's licensing exams to become registered dietitians, and are now employed full time helping people with their dietary needs. But there's a substantial difference in the lives of these two individuals. In order for Aaron to attend High Society University, he had to take out more than $100,000 in student loans. Sarah, on the other hand, qualified for work-study financial assistance and diligently worked all of the hours she could to keep her college expenses as low as possible. Oh, she still had to take out a student loan to complete her studies, but by attending the most affordable schools she could and working part time while taking classes, she was able to graduate owing only $14,000.

Aaron and Sarah now lead very different lives after graduating and entering the workforce. Aaron was able to secure an above-average starting salary of $45,000. He believes his high starting salary is a direct result of graduating from such a fine school, but he can't be certain. Even though he is starting his career with an above-average starting salary, he's struggling to make ends meet. His monthly student loan payments are so high that he can barely afford to make the payments in addition to his rent, utilities, groceries, and other living expenses. Despite securing a great starting salary, Aaron isn't prospering. He's so deep in debt that he's concerned about being able to buy a home of his own, upgrade his nearly worn out car, or even being able to scrape up enough money to take the occasional vacation. He may even have to postpone getting married until he can get his financial situation straightened out. And since it will probably take many years to pay down his student loans and work his way up in the company to secure a higher salary, who knows how long that will take?

Sarah was also able to secure a starting salary of $45,000. The same company that recruited Aaron at High Society University also recruited Sarah from her state university. In addition to her strong GPA and extracurricular activities, the company was also very impressed by the fact that she had worked part-time while in school through the work-study program. This proved to them that she was someone who had a strong work ethic – just the kind of candidate they look for. Sarah's student loan debt of $14,000 is low enough that her monthly payments are not a burden. Nevertheless, she plans on paying down this debt as soon as possible so she can start saving for a down payment on a home…but not before taking a much-deserved week-long vacation in Cancun with some friends to celebrate her graduation and new career.

The moral to my little parable is this: Graduating from an expensive school does not guarantee anything. In fact, if you end up with substantial student loan debt after earning a degree from an expensive school, your chances of getting a good start in life may be much lower than those who graduated from much more affordable schools. This is especially true for those careers that have a very defined salary range. Does it really make any sense to pay many times more for a college degree for a particular career if the average starting salary is the same whether you graduated from a big-name school or from a more affordable school? And consider this…many companies that recruit from expensive schools also recruit from state colleges and universities as well. They are often far more interested in finding the best candidates for the positions they need to fill than they are impressed by the name on your diploma.

Although there are many different ways to save money on college tuition and expenses, there are some that are very simple and easy to implement, such as attending community colleges and affordable in-state universities. Don't make the mistake of overlooking them. Let's go ahead now and take a closer look at several simple strategies you can use to save literally thousands of dollars in your pursuit of a college degree. These strategies represent low-hanging fruit that can be easily used in nearly any degree program, regardless of the school you intend to graduate from.

Community Colleges

If you've decided that you are definitely college-bound and the career path you are interested in requires a college degree, one of the first places to look for affordable college credit is your local community college. By attending a community college for your first two years you can easily save thousands of dollars. The lower-division courses community colleges offer are the same as those offered by four-year schools, except they are much more affordable. You can complete your first two years of college at a community college at a fraction of the cost of what you would otherwise spend at another school and then transfer the credits into a bachelor's degree program to graduate.

The first two years of a typical bachelor's degree are made up of a series of general education (gen ed) or lower-division courses. Community colleges usually offer all of the gen ed courses you'll need for much less than four-year schools charge for the same courses. Students who are residents of California, for example, have some of the most affordable community college tuition in the nation at just $36 per credit hour. These days most community colleges even have articulation agreements with local colleges and universities that guarantee you the ability to transfer 100 percent of your associate's degree into a bachelor's degree program.

How much money can you save by attending a community college instead of a four-year college or university for your first two years of college? Quite a bit. We're not talking about pocket change here, either. According to The College Board the average in-state community college tuition in the United States for 2012 was $2,960 per year while the average in-state tuition at a four-year state school is $8,240. And get this, the average in-state tuition at a private four-year school is $28,500. When you compare prices, it's not hard to see the community college advantage, is it? Let's see…you can attend a community college for nearly one-third the price of an in-state four-year school or nearly one-tenth the price of an in-state private school. I don't know about you but it's not a tough call for me to make.

If community colleges are such a great deal, why don't more people take advantage of them for their first two years of college and then transfer to a four-year school for their last two years to graduate? It's an issue of perception. Unfortunately, community colleges have managed to acquire the undeserved reputation of being easier or somehow less-prestigious than other schools. There are some who even go so far as to say that community colleges are not "real" colleges. This couldn't be further from the truth. This false perception probably originated at least in part from the open enrollment policies that community colleges have where they accept nearly everyone who applies. But just because a school has open enrollment doesn't necessarily mean that its courses and degree programs are easy.[2]

Let's take a closer look at the myth of community colleges being easier than other schools. First, it's important to realize that most college instructors develop their own courses. With rare exceptions, the job of developing courses falls in the hands of the same instructors who teach them. This means you can have a mix of both easy and difficult instructors at nearly any school, prestigious or not. The difficulty of each course is more a factor of each individual instructor than of a particular school.

Second, just because community colleges have open enrollment doesn't mean that everyone who applies actually graduates. In 2010 the Christian Science Monitor reported that about half of all community college students drop out after their first year. And of those who stick with the program, only 25 percent actually graduate. Just because a school has open enrollment does not mean that it is easy. The only thing that can be inferred from open enrollment is that more people are given a chance at higher education…that's all. The difficulty of the courses offered by community colleges does a fine job of weeding out

---

[2] To this day one of the most difficult college instructors I ever had was the guy who taught introductory Spanish courses at a community college I attended. Even though these were supposed to be "introductory" courses, he completely skipped over many of the basics that are taught in introductory foreign language courses and went straight into more complex topics. Positively. Brutal.

those who are not ready for the challenges of college-level learning.

Now that we've dispelled the myth of community colleges being easy, let's take a look at one major advantage community colleges have over large state and private universities (other than the obvious financial savings): Namely, small class sizes. If you attend a large university for your first two years, guess what? Many of the lower-division courses you take will be taught in large lecture halls that may have 100, 200, or more students each. Individualized attention from your instructor? Fugetaboutit. These classes are often so large that unless instructors take attendance (which many don't), they won't even notice you're not there if you suddenly come down with the flu and can't make it to class. And to make matters worse, many of these lower-division courses aren't even taught by professors with doctorates. These courses are often taught by teaching assistants with master's degrees while the actual professors at these research universities are off someplace else doing research. So, let's see…many people are willing to spend many times more than what community colleges charge to take classes that are taught in large lecture halls by teaching assistants instead of professors and they get very little (or no) individualized attention when needed…just so they can attend a school with more prestige. Does this make any sense to you?

Community colleges, on the other hand, almost always have small class sizes which makes it very easy to interact with your instructors. In addition, some of the instructors who teach at community colleges do so on a part-time basis. They often don't teach for the money, but rather, they teach because it's something they really enjoy. It's not just a paycheck to them. Many of these part-time instructors are professionals in the subjects they teach. A part-time business instructor, for example, may be a successful business owner. A part-time accounting instructor may be a CPA at a local accounting firm. And a part-time nursing instructor may be a nurse practitioner at a local clinic. Because many community college instructors are successful professionals who teach on a part-time basis, they can often offer special insights and certain perspectives on the subjects they teach that full-time instructors simply don't possess.

Okay, quiz time: What do community colleges and Chuck Yeager both have in common? Answer: They both have *the right stuff*. And if community colleges didn't have the right stuff, do you think four-year schools would accept credit from them in transfer? Of course not. In reality, these schools offer a high-quality education at a very affordable price. They are so affordable, in fact, that many people who qualify for the Pell Grant are able to attend community colleges at no cost whatsoever.

If you read through this book and your main takeaway from it is that you can save a bundle by attending a community college for your first two years of college, you can use that information alone to save thousands of dollars in tuition. Mission accomplished. It simply doesn't make any financial sense to take the same courses at a four-year school (state or private) and pay several times more for them.

Dual Enrollment (Two Birds – One Stone)

The gen ed courses that make up the first two years of a college degree are essentially a repeat of many of the courses you take in high school. Really, there's almost no difference in course content. High school and community college administrators know this and are more frequently making arrangements to award college credit through local community colleges for the completion of high school courses. These are known as dual enrollment courses.

If you are still in high school and your school offers dual enrollment courses, sign up for every one that's offered. There's no better way to kill two birds with one stone. Why take separate high school and college courses to cover the same material? It gets even better. The already low community college fees for dual enrollment credit are often substantially reduced for high school students. This makes an already great deal nearly impossible to pass up.

A fairly new trend in dual enrollment is the community college and high school hybrid. In these schools students graduate with both a high school diploma and an associate's degree at the same time. Now, we're not talking about super-students or over-achievers either, just average high school students. They don't even need to multitask or miss summer vacations to do it. Remember, most gen ed courses have essentially the same content as high school courses. Enlightened school officials all across the nation are now making the dual enrollment opportunity a reality for many students. This dramatically shortens the path to earning a college degree and saves a lot of money at the same time.

Another major advantage of earning college credit while still in high school (aside from the financial savings) is that you can skip entrance exams when applying to many bachelor's degree programs. If you accumulate at least 30 credit hours of college credit while in high school, entrance exams are no longer required at many colleges and universities. You simply apply as a transfer student, stand on the merits of your college grades, and kiss studying for the SAT or ACT goodbye. The purpose of college entrance exams is to assess a particular student's readiness for college-level learning. Nothing less, nothing more.

After acquiring at least 30 credit hours of college credits, there is no longer any need for such entrance exams. Potential schools are able to make an adequate assessment of your future abilities based on the college credits you've already acquired.

Tuition Money From Your Employer

Many people are often surprised to learn that the company they work for offers money that can be used to take college courses. The amount varies with different companies but somewhere around $5,000 per year is the average. This is money that does not have to be repaid. It's considered an employee benefit the same as health insurance, retirement, and vacation time. Most larger companies offer this benefit although few people ever take advantage of it.

Employers that offer tuition money as a benefit usually do so as a reimbursement for a course after it has been completed. You will have to pay for your courses up front but you can apply for reimbursement after you have completed them to a satisfactory level. A grade of at least a "C" for each course will usually do.

Each company will have its own policy on tuition reimbursement so check with your human resources department for details. Typically, someone at the management level will have to sign off on the courses you would like to be reimbursed for before you enroll. It makes sense to get a written approval before enrolling anyway since it guarantees you will be reimbursed for your courses after you've finished them. Approved courses are typically those the company thinks will improve job performance. Gen ed courses are usually approved as well as upper-level courses in your field of work. However, if you work in marketing and request approval for nursing, engineering, or any other courses that are totally unrelated to your job, this might raise your manager's suspicions a bit. If management suspects you are using employee tuition assistance to prepare for a career change, you may be denied reimbursement approval.

Shop Around for the Best Deal

When you are in the market for a new computer, washing machine, or perhaps a new car, do you buy the first one you see? I don't. I shop around for the best deals, check out different stores' prices, look at different brands, and even try them out. Yet, this is what many people do when it comes to choosing a college. They may choose a school because it's close to home, has a great sports team, or perhaps it's where the family has always gone to school. Oddly, price is not usually one of the main factors people use to choose a school. Typically, a person will choose a school and then try to figure out how to pay for it. This is the opposite of how the process should work.

The Internet is truly the great equalizer when it comes to shopping for an affordable school. Prior to the Internet, you would have to either write, call, or visit to get the information you needed to make an informed decision. Today, you can get all the information you need on many different schools just by going online. One of the best places on the web to start your search is Geteducated.com where you can check out the rankings of most affordable schools.

Do your homework before deciding on a school. Know what the costs are before making a commitment. Compare costs, transfer policies, and graduation requirements. And by all means, shop around for the best deal.

Go Online and Save Big Money

In just the past few years a new method of delivering college courses has shaken the higher education establishment – online courses for college credit. Online learning is now so common that it's quite a challenge to find a school that doesn't offer online courses.

Online learning allows you to take courses on your home computer with an Internet connection from anywhere in the world. You no longer have to worry about getting to class on time, commuting to class, or missing that all-too-important exam due to a scheduling conflict. Online courses also enable you to work full time and continue to earn college credit in the evenings, mornings, nights, or whenever you have free time. The academic studies that have been conducted on the effectiveness of online learning always have the same results – online courses are just as effective as classroom-based courses. There's no significant difference in learning outcomes.[3]

To give you an idea of just how mainstream online learning has become, the following is a small sample of schools that either offer online courses or entire degree programs that can be completed online:

- Harvard University
- Stanford University
- Duke University
- The University of Florida (Go Gators!)

---

[3] Thomas L. Russell, of North Carolina State University, compiled data from 355 research reports in his book, "The No Significant Difference Phenomenon," where researchers could not identify any significant difference in learning outcomes between those who took classes in person and those who completed them from a distance.

- The University of Connecticut
- Cornell University
- The University of California – Berkeley
- Auburn University
- The University of Alabama
- Pennsylvania State University

Clearly, online courses and degree programs are here to stay. With the Internet you are no longer geographically limited to a school in your neighborhood.

The best part of online learning is the ability to shop around for the most affordable sources of college credit, regardless of where the school is located. What if the school is on the other side of the country? It doesn't matter. You won't need to visit it for any reason.

Not all schools require that you be enrolled in a degree program to take online courses. There are some that will allow you to take a few courses to use as transfer credit to another school. It's not unreasonable to take affordable online courses from one or more schools, transfer them into a degree program and then complete the last 30 credit hours through a particular school to graduate. An entire chapter of this book is devoted to online and independent study courses where you will discover some of the most affordable sources of college credit there is.

Saving Money on College Textbooks

Tuition isn't the only major expense you'll encounter in your pursuit of a college degree. Another major expense that usually doesn't get much attention is the cost of textbooks. Most textbooks these days cost $100, $200, or more each. After taking several courses, this can really add up to a sizable pile of money. Textbooks for full-time students can easily cost $1,000 or more per semester. Thankfully, there's a simple solution to this expensive problem.

First of all, don't buy your books from the school bookstore. They're overpriced, even the used ones. Find out which books will be required for the courses you are taking. In addition to the title, author, and edition, be sure to get the book's ISBN number. The ISBN number is a type of identification number used by publishing companies and is usually found on the back cover of the book. Sometimes this information can be found online in the course description or you can contact the instructor. Don't count on the school bookstore to give you this information. If they suspect you're going to get the book from another source, they may clam up. After all, the school bookstore is a business and must generate a profit, the same as any other store. They aren't selling books for the fun of it.

The next step is to pull up a search engine in your computer's Internet browser (any good search engine will do) and enter the ISBN number. You will then get links to various companies selling the book used for substantially less than the new price. Spend some time checking out these different companies. Some will have better prices than others. Find the best deal and go with it.

Okay, so you got a great deal on the purchase of your book and have now finished the course. What do you do with it now? Let it collect dust on a bookshelf? Sell it used to the school bookstore? In most cases school bookstores offer very little for used books. It's usually not even worth checking with them. However, with the power of the Internet, you can sell your book online and recoup most (sometimes all) of your investment. The best company to do this with is Amazon since it allows anyone to list used books for sale. You can see the prices others are charging for the same book and price yours to sell.

If you buy your books used from online vendors and then sell them used when your courses are finished, college textbooks no longer have to be a financial burden. I have personally used this simple strategy many times to obtain textbooks for mere pennies on the dollar. Nearly every time I was able to resell my textbooks online and recoup more than 90 percent of my initial investment (and occasionally closer to 100 percent). To ensure you get the most money for your used textbooks, be sure you list them for sale just as soon as your courses are over (assuming your courses are semester based). The timing is important. Demand for college textbooks is greatest during that brief period in between semesters when everyone is rushing to get the textbooks they need for their new courses. You can get the most money for your books if you list them for sale during this brief window. This also ensures a quick sale.

Consider Renting Instead of Buying

Another strategy you can use to save big on college textbooks is to completely skip buying them. Just rent them instead. There are now several online textbook rental companies that make the rental process very easy. The rental fees these companies charge are (usually) much lower than what you would pay to purchase the same books. A simple internet search for "textbook rental" turns up many great options to choose from.

If you are considering renting textbooks, it's important to compare companies' rental prices to the cost of purchasing used textbooks online before making a commitment. From time to time you may encounter a situation where it is actually cheaper to purchase a particular textbook used instead of renting it, although this is rare.

Although you can definitely realize substantial savings by renting textbooks over buying new at the school bookstore, you are probably not going to save as much money with this strategy as you would by purchasing used textbooks online and then reselling them online to recoup most of your investment. Nevertheless, renting is far more preferable than buying new and is ideal for those who don't want to have to deal with selling their books after their courses are over.

Just Scratching the Surface

There you go. We're only on the second chapter and you've already seen some very simple and practical strategies you can use to dramatically lower the cost of earning a college degree. But really, at this point we've only begun to scratch the surface of what's possible. In the next three chapters we'll take a look at a few schools that don't even charge any tuition.

Come again? No tuition?

It's true. Did you know such schools even existed? Let's check them out…

CHAPTER 3

Hard Work University

"If A equals success, then the formula is A = X + Y + Z. Where X is work. Y is play. Z is keep your mouth shut."

– Albert Einstein

In a perfect world we would simply enroll in a college that doesn't charge any tuition. Such a college would also provide us with a part-time job and would work closely with us to make sure we graduate with little or no debt. And in other news, the fountain of youth has just been discovered in the city of El Dorado and is being guarded by a group of little green men riding unicorns. Although it's easy to scoff at the idea of a tuition-free college, the concept for such a school isn't a fantasy – they really do exist. Let's take a look at four of these free schools. Let's take a look at the work colleges.

There are seven colleges that are collectively referred to as "work colleges." Three of them don't charge any tuition while the other four do. For our purposes the work colleges that charge tuition will be ignored. The tuition-free colleges in the Work College Consortium (www.workcolleges.org) are Alice Lloyd College, Berea College, and College of the Ozarks. There's another college that, while technically not part of the Work College Consortium, operates in a similar manner. This school is Deep Springs College. We'll take a good look at it as well.

The work college concept is simple. All students are required to work anywhere from 10 to 20 hours per week, regardless of their financial backgrounds. The work is mandatory; there are no exceptions. Students do the work in exchange for free tuition and to eliminate other expenses. They are also paid a small wage for their work after tuition and other expenses are deducted. Although room and board is not free at the work colleges, financial assistance is provided to many students who attend these schools to cover their living expenses so that they can truly graduate with a debt-free college degree.

The student work requirement at the work colleges allows them to keep their expenses lower than other schools by needing fewer full-time personnel. Ironically, there used to be many colleges in the United States where work was a component of the educational and financial aid process. This is truly curious since headlines of the ever-increasing costs of higher education are frequently making the news. Perhaps a return to the work college model for many schools is the answer to such skyrocketing costs. Surely, hard work is not a thing of the past, is it?

Earn While You Learn

The work requirement is not just a way to eliminate the expenses associated with earning a college degree. The work colleges consider the work requirement to be just as much a part of the educational process as traditional academic work. The work requirement builds character, instills a strong work ethic, and teaches many skills that students would otherwise only learn later in life. The type of work students perform varies a great deal, from such common jobs as yard work, food service, maintenance, and others to some truly interesting jobs that may have students working on a farm, at a historic hotel, in a greenhouse, or making crafts.

First-year students are typically assigned jobs. It's almost unheard of for first-year students to have any say in the types of jobs they are given. Second-year students, however, *may* have the option to apply for jobs that are more relevant to their personal interests or majors. Just as it is in the job market after graduation, landing the best jobs at the work colleges is not easy. These jobs are competitive and have many applicants.

The amount of money students earn from their jobs is usually equivalent to the minimum wage. Part of the wages are retained by the colleges to offset tuition and other expenses with students receiving the remainder to spend on personal needs. Each of the work colleges has a different method of paying students for their work. Some issue periodic paychecks while others issue lump-sum payments directly to students' accounts once per year.

Even though all students are required to work, it's definitely possible to be fired from a job. This could be caused by any number of things such as showing up late, poor performance, insubordination, or any other thing that could cause someone to be fired from a regular job. If a work college student is fired from a job, he will have to apply for another job in a different department. Failure to maintain consistent employment may be grounds for dismissal from school.

Alice Lloyd College

Located in the beautiful Appalachian Mountains of eastern Kentucky in the small community of Pippa Passes, Alice

Lloyd College (www.alc.edu) has been offering a high-quality (and free) education since its founding in 1923. Originally known as Caney Junior College and later renamed after its founder, the school awarded associate's degrees until 1982 when it became a four-year college. Although Alice Lloyd College (ALC) primarily enrolls students who are from the Appalachian Mountains, students from outside the region and even international students are accepted as well.

Alice Lloyd College is a very small school with just over 600 students, none of whom pay any tuition. Private donations cover many of the school's expenses. Alice Lloyd College also doesn't accept any direct federal or state funding although it does accept the Pell Grant from students who qualify. Most of Alice Lloyd's students enroll immediately after high school although transfer students are accepted as well. Up to 64 credit hours may be transferred in from regionally accredited two-year schools and as many as 90 credit hours from four-year schools.

Alice Lloyd College's student work program has been an important part of the educational experience and student financial aid since it was founded. In the school's earliest days, students participated in almost every conceivable job that needed doing. The pioneering new students even helped in the construction of their own educational facilities. Today the jobs are much more structured. Students are required to work an average of 10 hours per week or a total of 160 hours per semester. Typical jobs include grounds and facilities maintenance, custodian, resident adviser, food services at the Hunger Din, lifeguard, library assistant, academic assistant, computer technician, daycare worker, radio station technician, and many others. To spice things up a bit the school holds an annual work awards ceremony that recognizes outstanding job performance from each work area. Another popular annual event is the Student Work Olympics where students from each work area compete in several fun games for a prize consisting of a pizza party for the victors. Who says it has to be all work and no play?

The opportunities offered by Alice Lloyd College don't end after you've graduated and hung your diploma on the wall. If you are a graduate of ALC and are accepted into a graduate degree program at the University of Kentucky, you can apply to stay at Caney Cottage, an apartment complex owned by ALC, where you can stay rent and utilities free while completing your graduate degree. In addition, ALC graduates who go on to pursue a graduate degree from any school *may* qualify to have their graduate degrees funded by ALC in exchange for serving in the Appalachian Mountains in their chosen professions after graduating.

Alice Lloyd College represents an incredible opportunity to earn a bachelor's degree without accumulating any debt. Alice Lloyd herself would no doubt be very proud of how the college she founded has grown and matured. Her original vision of creating a thriving academic community that doesn't financially burden its students continues to this day and has a very bright future in the years to come.

Berea College

Berea College (www.berea.edu) is a vibrant liberal arts college located in the small town of Berea, Kentucky, not far from the city of Lexington. Among its many distinctions, Berea College was the first interracial and coeducational college in the south when it was founded in 1855. The school also consistently ranks as the number one liberal arts college in the south year after year in the most respected lists of college rankings. Berea College doesn't charge any tuition to any of its students. Like Alice

Lloyd College, Berea College primarily seeks to enroll students who are from the Appalachian Mountains, although students from throughout the nation and other countries are accepted as well.

Berea College is ideally located for those who enjoy the arts. The town of Berea is a small community where many artisans and craftsmen have made their home. There are so many artisans in Berea, in fact, that the town has been designated the Official Folk, Arts, and Crafts Capital of Kentucky. The town is a popular tourist destination and holds several arts and crafts festivals each year.

Berea College offers bachelors degrees in many different fields of study. The school has a remarkably low student-to-faculty ratio of just 10 to 1 and a student body of nearly 1,600 which makes it very easy to get to know and interact with your professors and other students. Berea College also encourages students to participate in international study. Nearly half of the school's students participate in a study abroad program prior to graduating.

Berea's student work program is the key to keeping costs low so that all of its students can receive a free education. Students work an average of 10 hours per week, although it's possible to work more hours with special permission. During the summer months students can work full-time on campus or in intern positions off campus. Students progress through a series of "grade levels" as they move from job to job. All freshmen are assigned a Grade One job. Subsequent jobs teach new skills and have new responsibilities. Many senior-level students end up in supervisory positions where they train and oversee newer students.

Not all of Berea's available jobs are on its campus. Some assignments are off-campus in the community. Typical jobs include teaching assistant, resident adviser, administrative support, custodian, maintenance, yard work, library and bookstore assistant, and others. Berea College has some very interesting and unique jobs as well. The college owns Boone Tavern, a historic hotel and restaurant, which is staffed primarily with students. The college also owns its own student-operated crafts shop where students learn many new skills as they make crafts from wood, cloth, pottery, and metal. These crafts are sold to the general public to help fund the school (www.bereacollegecrafts.com).

Berea College is truly a great school in every way. Students earn a first-rate education, are surrounded by a community of artisans in a charming small town, are encouraged to participate in international study, and most importantly, have the opportunity to earn a debt-free college degree.

College of the Ozarks

College of the Ozarks (www.cofo.edu) is located less than five miles south of the popular vacation town of Branson, Missouri, on a beautiful 1,000 acre campus. The college provides a tuition-free education to all of its 1,600 students who aren't afraid of a little hard work. In fact, the school refers to itself as "Hard Work U," a nickname the administration, faculty, and students are all very proud of.

College of the Ozarks was originally founded in 1907 as a high school in an area of the country where few high schools existed. In its earliest days it was known simply as The School of the Ozarks. From the very beginning students were expected to work in exchange for tuition. In 1956 the school transitioned to a two-year college and in 1965 it became a four-year college. College of the Ozarks accepts 300-350 new students each year for the fall term. Transfer students with a minimum GPA of 3.0 are also accepted; however, if you have earned more than 60 credit hours, you may no longer qualify for admission.

The student work program at College of the Ozarks has been in place since the school's earliest days as a high school. Students are required to work at least 15 hours per week to cover tuition and other expenses. Many of the on-campus jobs are fairly typical but there are also several unique and interesting jobs that students can hold as well.

College of the Ozarks has the distinction of having its own museum on the campus grounds and is one of the more interesting places where students can work. Within the walls of the three-story Ralph Foster Museum are many fascinating artifacts from the Ozarks region including Native American artifacts, western antiques, natural history artifacts, and many others. One of the museum's most popular exhibits is the original 1921 Oldsmobile truck used in "The Beverly Hillbillies" television series.

Another interesting place where students can work is the Fruitcake and Jelly Kitchen. This truly unique establishment has been producing fruitcakes, jellies, preservatives, apple butter, and other delicacies since 1934. Fruitcakes are now the Kitchen's main seller and it makes more than 40,000 of them each year to meet demand (so *that's* where they all come from!).

The Edwards Mill is yet another interesting place where students can work. The mill is powered by a large water wheel that grinds meal and flour and houses work areas where students weave rugs, shawls, baskets, and other items that are available for sale to the public.

There are many other interesting work opportunities available for students to pursue. Students can work in the school's large greenhouse, at a dairy, or even at a 30-room log cabin-style lodge and conference center. There is truly no shortage of interesting and unique jobs for students at College of the Ozarks!

College of the Ozarks students really do have it all. Free tuition, unique job opportunities, and proximity to a popular tourist town are the perfect combination for a great education, a debt-free degree, and many great college memories.

Deep Springs College

One of the most unique colleges in the nation is found in the desert community of Deep Springs, California, just minutes from the Nevada border. Imagine a school where you live and work on an isolated cattle ranch with two dozen other "ranch hands." Your day starts very early in the morning as you don your cowboy hat and tend to chores around the ranch. You might find yourself cooking breakfast for the crew, herding cattle, maintaining the school's grounds, or taking care of any number of other things that need attention. With your morning chores now complete, you head to class for a few hours. Your classes are very small with only seven or eight students in each one. With such small classes you are able to engage in lively discussions with your professors and classmates, a perfect environment for learning. As evening approaches, a spontaneous game of Frisbee breaks out amongst some students while others spend time planning an upcoming hiking and climbing excursion to the nearby High Sierras. The rest of your evening is spent preparing for the next day's classes. Welcome to Deep Springs College.

Deep Springs College (www.deepsprings.edu) is a prestigious two-year school established in 1917 for men. No admitted students pay any tuition, room, or board. Although Deep Springs was originally established as an all-male school, female students are now accepted as well. One of the more unique aspects of Deep Springs is the school's tiny student body, which consists of about 25 students at any given time. The school's students also have no trouble choosing a major since only one degree program is offered, an associate's degree in liberal arts. As an elite two-year college, the majority of Deep Springs' students transfer to and graduate from some of the most prestigious universities in the nation including Stanford, Harvard, Yale, Brown, and others.

The Deep Springs College "campus" is very remote. The near-total isolation from the outside world is considered an asset since it allows students to concentrate fully on their studies and work. Being very close to the California and Nevada border, the closest town to Deep Springs College is actually 25 miles away in Nevada. Although cell phone reception is nonexistent due to the isolated campus location, students do have access to high-speed Internet and television via satellite.

One of the more noteworthy aspects of Deep Springs College is not what it has, but rather, what is missing when compared to other colleges. There are no clubs, organized sports teams, special events, or any of the usual extracurricular activities one would normally expect at a college. Instead, students essentially have to create their own entertainment. There isn't a lot of free time at the college but many students like to relax by throwing around a ball or Frisbee, listening to music, watching a movie, or exploring the surrounding desert.

Deep Springs College is very much a working cattle ranch. Students tend to the cattle herd, the school's alfalfa farm, and take care of the many other jobs that make life in the desert possible. Students work a minimum of 20 hours per week in jobs that are straight out of an Old West movie.

Such job titles as cowboy, feed person, butcher, and others may seem out of place at most colleges but are common at Deep Springs College. Unlike the work colleges, the work requirement at Deep Springs College is not for the purpose of eliminating student debt. Rather, the work requirement is considered an integral part of the students' education. Tuition, room, and board are covered by the school's endowment.

Admission to Deep Springs College is highly competitive and only 11 to 15 new students are accepted each year from an applicant pool of nearly 200. The admissions process itself is very much nonstandard and involves a group consisting of the school's professors and students gathering to review and vote on each applicant. Students who make the first cut are invited to spend several days on campus where they will be interviewed and have a chance to participate in the cowboy lifestyle and ranch chores.

Deep Springs College offers a truly unique opportunity to study under top-notch professors and obtain valuable experience in both work and life. It is a place where lifelong friendships are sure to be made due to the small, close-knit community. If your high school grades and test scores are competitive, don't overlook this great opportunity to earn the first two years of a bachelor's degree without accumulating any debt. The experiences you'll have as a ranch hand alone are worth it. Just think of all the stories of adventure you'll get to tell your kids and grand kids.

Working your way through college in exchange for free tuition – what a concept! Isn't a shame there aren't more schools like these? There are hundreds of small colleges all over the map that would make ideal work colleges. All it takes is the right leadership to make it happen. If you believe you have the right qualifications for any of the work colleges, you should definitely apply. Earning a college degree in something that leads to a solid career is always a good thing but earning a degree and graduating completely debt-free, now that's priceless!

We're not finished with schools that don't charge any tuition. In the next chapter we'll take a look at three truly unique schools you can attend where you can earn a college degree in several different areas of study. Like the work colleges, these schools don't charge any tuition; however, they do charge room and board. Nevertheless, by not having to deal with the most expensive part of earning a college degree (high tuition), you can still come out ahead of your peers by attending one of these schools.

CHAPTER 4

Tuition-Free Is the Way to Be

"Live within your means, never be in debt, and by husbanding your money you can always lay it out well. But when you get in debt you become a slave. Therefore I say to you never involve yourself in debt, and become no man's surety."

– Andrew Jackson

Colleges that don't charge any tuition are not limited to the work colleges (did you realize there were so many of these schools?). There are two colleges in the United States that have a highly specialized focus and curriculum that primarily concentrate on educating students for a particular career or profession. These two schools are Curtis Institute of Music and Webb Institute. These schools train students for careers in musical performing arts, engineering, and ship design. And there's another school, Macaulay Honors College, that offers a broad-based curriculum in the liberal arts. Although these schools don't charge any tuition to their accepted students, none of them cover room and board. Students are on their own in this area. Nevertheless, by not having to deal with tuition, the savings students can realize over other schools are substantial and should not be ignored.

Macaulay Honors College

Are you a resident of the state of New York? If so, you should definitely take a look at the Macaulay Honors College (http://macaulay.cuny.edu), a unique school in New York for academically gifted students. It is a school that offers full-tuition scholarships (for four years of undergraduate study) to all students who are accepted, in addition to a few other perks. Approximately 1,200 students are enrolled in the program. Although Macaulay students do not have to pay any tuition, they are responsible for room and board in addition to any additional fees they may incur, such as student activity fees, late fees, and others.

Macaulay Honors College was founded in 2001 as a way to reward high-achieving students who are studying at several institutions within the City University of New York (the largest urban university system in the nation). In addition to not having to worry about tuition for their undergraduate studies, Macaulay students are also given a free Apple laptop computer, a special pass for either free or reduced admissions at various cultural, educational, and arts functions in New York City, and may also qualify for a $7,500 grant for internships and other learning opportunities outside the traditional classroom.

Although Macaulay has its own small "campus", which consists of one building, students take the majority of their classes at one of eight City University of New York (CUNY) colleges. Participating CUNY colleges include Baruch College, Brooklyn College, City College, Hunter College, John Jay College, Lehman College, Queens College, and College of Staten Island. Macaulay students officially graduate with a dual degree from both their "home" college and the Macaulay Honors College.

Macaulay Honors College represents an incredible opportunity to earn a debt-free degree for those high-achieving students who are residents of the state of New York. If this describes you, why not check out this great program to see if you qualify?

Curtis Institute of Music

Established in 1924 and located in Philadelphia, Pennsylvania, Curtis Institute of Music (www.curtis.edu) offers tuition-free degrees in the musical performing arts. The conservatory was established by wealthy publishing heiress and music aficionado, Mary Louise Curtis Bok, who gave the school a generous endowment to ensure its continuation and so that its students would not have to pay any tuition. The school's sole purpose is to train highly talented musicians to enter lifelong careers as professional musicians. Curtis Institute of Music maintains a student body of approximately 160 students, which is just enough for a full orchestra and a separate opera department.

Curtis Institute of Music offers a diploma, a bachelor of music, a master of music in opera, and a professional studies certificate in opera. Departments of study include music composition, conducting, instruments, and vocal studies.

In 2011 Curtis Institute opened a new facility, Lenfest Hall. This new building doubled the size of the school's campus and provides housing for half of the school's students. First and second year students are required to stay in Lenfest Hall while third and fourth year students live in off-campus housing.

Learning by Doing

Earning college credits at Curtis Institute of Music may take longer than a typical semester in some instances. Although the school uses the traditional method of accumulating college credits to graduate, many of these credits are not earned until a student's performance is acceptable to her teachers. Although the average student spends four years at the school, some students take longer to graduate. The school gives around 100 public concerts each year to further its teaching philosophy of "learning by doing" and to generate community interest.

The way Curtis Institute of Music maintains its staff of instructors is also somewhat nonstandard when compared to other schools. Instead of hiring full-time instructors, as most schools do, many of Curtis Institute's staff are professional musicians who teach on a part-time basis. Not only does this allow for substantial savings in salary and benefits, but the students also benefit by being exposed to many different instructors with a variety of talents and techniques.

Competitive Entry for a Rewarding Career

Admission to Curtis Institute is highly competitive. In fact, the school accepts a smaller percentage of applicants each year than the famous Juilliard School. Applicants must complete a formal application, submit standardized test scores, and make a trip to Philadelphia for a live audition. The school does not accept video or audio recordings in lieu of in-person auditions.

Many of Curtis Institute of Music's alumni go on to have careers in some of the most prestigious orchestras in the world. If you are a talented, passionate musician and are considering a career in this field, Curtis Institute of Music should be at the top of your list of potential schools.

Webb Institute

Established in 1889 in New York State and located in the Long Island community of Glen Cove, Webb Institute (www.webb-institute.edu) offers tuition-free degrees in naval architecture and marine engineering. The school is located on 26 acres and is housed in an early 1900's mansion with its own private beach.

Webb Institute's mansion is not just a school; it's also a movie star. In fact, you've probably seen it on the silver screen in the movie *Batman Forever* as Bruce Wayne's estate. It also appeared in the 1998 movie adaptation of *Great Expectations*. The mansion houses both classrooms and dorms; male dorms are in the mansion while female dorms are in an adjacent building. The school has a student body of around 90 students and a staff of 10 full-time instructors.

A Unique School for a Unique Mission

Webb Institute is a truly unique school that was created to fill a very specific niche. It was established by shipbuilder William Henry Webb to advance the science and design of naval ships. Webb provided the school with a generous endowment to enable its continuation and to provide a solid education to its students so that they wouldn't have to be burdened with tuition. Webb Institute's engineering degree program is accredited by the Accreditation Board for Engineering and Technology (ABET), the gold standard of engineering accreditation in the United States.

Webb Institute's students have never had any trouble choosing a major since only one undergraduate degree program is offered, a bachelor of science in naval architecture and marine engineering. Even though only one engineering degree is offered, students in the school's program don't have to worry about a lack of career opportunities if they later decide that designing ships is not their thing. Although the degree program is primarily designed to train new professionals in the ship design industry, it is really a hybrid engineering degree that also includes courses in systems engineering, electrical engineering, mechanical engineering, structural engineering, and civil engineering. Many Webb Institute graduates have gone on to earn graduate degrees in other engineering disciplines and have established careers that are very different from the school's maritime focus. If grad school is not in a student's immediate plans after graduation, obtaining a job in ship design is not a problem. Because of the school's unique focus and the lack of similar programs offered by other schools, Webb Institute graduates are in very high demand and the job placement rate is a remarkable 100 percent.

Like most engineering schools, academics at Webb Institute are intense. Each semester students take a full course load of challenging courses in mathematics, science, engineering, or ship design and are also required to take one humanities course each semester. It is common for students to spend hours in the classroom during the day and then have long evenings and nights working on assignments. In consideration of the long study hours that students put in, the school maintains a well-equipped library that is open 24 hours a day.

Assignments in many of Webb Institute's ship design courses are frequently in the form of challenging ship design projects. Students have access to everything they need to build and test their designs including well-equipped machine and carpentry shops and other laboratory facilities, including a 27 meter-long pool that was designed specifically to conduct hydrodynamic tests on ship models.

All Webb Institute students must participate in a mandatory internship during January and February of each year where they obtain practical experience working in some aspect of the maritime industry. A total of eight months of internship is necessary to graduate. Freshmen are typically assigned jobs at a shipyard, sophomores are placed on merchant ships, and juniors and seniors are placed in ship design offices. Although the internships each year are brief, they are paid positions, giving students an opportunity to earn some money during this time. Intern placements are typically in locations throughout the United States but can be in international locations as well.

It's Not All Work and No Play

Although students at Webb Institute spend a lot of time on their studies, there are still plenty of fun things to do outside of the classroom. Student life at the school is not all work and no play. Occasionally, a spontaneous game of ultimate Frisbee or football is started amongst the students right on the campus grounds. Other popular recreational activities include participation in intercollegiate sports, and since Webb Institute is right on the beach, sailing is a very popular pastime as well. If students need a break from the campus scene, they can visit nearby New York City for unlimited big-city entertainment. Students also have free unlimited access to the local YMCA to stay in shape and to work off any extra weight they may gain from the school's chef-prepared meals.

Although tuition at Webb Institute is free, students must still pay for their own room, board, books, and any additional supplies they may need. Students are required to reside on campus the entire four years of their studies, allowing for substantial savings over apartment expenses.

To be admitted to Webb Institute, a student must either be a United States citizen or have already obtained legal permanent residence. In addition to submitting the traditional college application and test scores, all applicants must travel to the campus for an in-person interview. No previously earned college credits may be transferred in as the school requires all students to start out as freshmen with a clean slate. Applicants must also pass a physical fitness test to ensure they are capable of meeting the demands of the required internships.

If you are someone who is interested in pursuing a career in engineering or if a career in ship design "floats your boat," you really can't go wrong with Webb Institute. The school is highly respected, has a small student body for a lot of individualized attention, and the free tuition is icing on the cake.

Even More Tuition-Free Schools Coming Up

We're still not finished exploring all of the schools in the United States that don't charge any tuition. In the next chapter we'll take a look at five top-notch schools that offer a variety of degree programs that don't burden their students with tuition, room, or board. These schools are the United States Service Academies and were created to prepare new officers for all branches of the U.S. military.

CHAPTER 5

The United States Service Academies

"The things taught in schools and colleges are not an education, but the means to an education."

– Ralph Waldo Emerson

Five More Great Options

Tuition-free colleges are not limited to the work colleges or the three schools discussed in the previous chapter. The United States government operates five schools that do not charge tuition, room, or board for any students who are accepted. The purpose of these schools is to educate and train new commissioned officers for each branch of the U.S. military. Collectively, they are referred to as the United States Service Academies. The Service Academies include the United States Merchant Marine Academy (Kings Point), the United States Military Academy (West Point), the United States Naval Academy (Annapolis), the United States Coast Guard Academy, and the United States Air Force Academy. All of the Service Academies are co-educational.

In exchange for free tuition, room, and board, and to fulfill the express mission of creating new commissioned officers, students of the U.S. Service Academies are obligated to serve in one branch of the United States military for a specified period of time after graduation. Students who graduate from West Point, Annapolis, the U.S. Coast Guard Academy, and the U.S. Air Force Academy are obligated to serve a minimum of five years of active duty in addition to three years of reserve duty. Students who graduate from Kings Point are obligated to serve up to eight years and may choose either a civilian or military career path. Service Academy graduates who pursue certain military career paths may end up with longer service obligations. Graduates of the U.S. Air Force Academy who become pilots, for example, must agree to a minimum service obligation of 10 years. It takes a lot of money and resources to train competent pilots and the U.S. Air Force wants to make sure it gets its money's worth with long service obligations.

With the exception of Kings Point, all Service Academy students are considered to be on active duty from their first day as students. Kings Point is excluded from this since it falls under the jurisdiction of the Department of Transportation. The academies for the Army, Navy, and Air Force are under the jurisdiction of the Department of Defense while the academy for the Coast Guard is under the Department of Homeland Security. The U.S. Marine Corps, which does not have an academy, commissions officers from both Annapolis and Kings Point.

U.S. Service Academy Admissions 101

To even be considered for admission to one of the U.S. Service Academies, with the exception of the U.S. Coast Guard Academy, potential students must obtain a nomination by one of the following:

- The Vice President of the United States
- A U.S. Congressman
- A U.S. Senator
- The Governors of Puerto Rico or American Samoa
- The Resident Commissioners of Puerto Rico or the Northern Mariana Islands
- Delegates from Washington, D.C., Guam, or the U.S. Virgin Islands
- The Secretary of the Army

Kings Point will only accept a nomination by a Senator or Congressman. The U.S. Coast Guard Academy does not require a nomination nor will they accept one; potential students must stand on the merits of their academic records and achievements.

Although obtaining such a nomination can be challenging, it's certainly not impossible. As long as you have solid grades and you don't have any skeletons in your closet, you should be considered. It's important to realize, however, that nominations are not automatic, nor is there any guarantee you will get one. Those who have the power to confer a nomination are only able to nominate a certain number of people each year. As such, you will be competing with others for a coveted nomination.

If you are serious about applying to one of the Service Academies, it's best to begin the process of securing a nomination as early as possible. If you are still in high school, you can begin the process prior to your senior year. The best approach to take for securing a nomination is to send nomination requests to every person who is qualified to nominate you. Don't be shy…get those nomination requests out there.

It's perfectly fine to use the same nomination request letter and address it to different people. Your letter needs to be very cordial and succinct; the correct use of grammar is a must. Avoid the use of slang and any unnecessary jargon and keep the letter brief and to the point. Tell them a little about yourself, why you want to go to one of the Service Academies, why you believe you are qualified to attend, and why you will be an asset while there and in your future military career. Be sure to include your grade point average and any extracurricular and community activities you have participated in.

After obtaining a nomination to attend one of the Service Academies, it's possible that you may receive a conditional acceptance proposal which requires you to attend a special preparatory school before being fully admitted to the academy. If this happens, don't despair. In fact, it's time to celebrate! You're in! And not only that, but you will be in good company, too. Many graduates of the Service Academy prep schools have gone on to become Rhodes Scholars, generals, astronauts, and to achieve many other noteworthy accomplishments. Being accepted to a Service Academy prep school is not a bad thing at all.

Each one of the Service Academies has its own prep school. There is no need to submit a separate application to both an academy and its prep school. If you are not accepted to the Service Academy you applied to, your application automatically defaults for prep school review. Each one of the prep schools offers a 10-month program where students engage in rigorous academic, physical, and military training. Admission to a Service Academy after graduating from one of the prep schools is not automatic, however; it depends upon your success as a prep school student.

The United States Merchant Marine Academy

The United States Merchant Marine Academy (www.usmma.edu), also known as Kings Point, is tasked with the creation of new officers for the U.S. Merchant Marine fleet as well as the U.S. military. The academy is located in Kings Point, New York, 20 miles from New York City, and has approximately 950 students and 250 staff. Kings Point does not charge tuition, room, or board to any accepted students.

The U.S. Merchant Marine fleet (in case you're wondering) is a fleet of civilian merchant ships that routinely transports various types of products and passengers on the open seas. However, the fleet is not just about transporting cars, televisions, and people from point A to point B. The fleet has an alter ego of sorts, kind of like Peter Parker and Spiderman, and leads an exciting double life. During a time of war the U.S. Merchant Marine fleet falls under the command of the U.S. Navy and is used to transport military personnel and supplies to war zones.

A School with a Rich History

The creation of Kings Point was the direct result of a fatal fire aboard a passenger ship in 1934 which resulted in the loss of 134 lives. In an effort to prevent such an occurrence from happening again, Congress passed the Merchant Marine Act of 1936 which regulated domestic maritime transportation companies and required ships to be manned by trained personnel. This laid the foundation for an academy with a formal program of study to graduate competent officers for commerce ships that fly the United States flag. Only two years after the passage of the Merchant Marine Act of 1936, the Merchant Marine Cadet Corps was established and a permanent home for the program with a new facility was later dedicated in 1943 in Kings Point, New York.

Of the five U.S. Service Academies, the U.S. Merchant Marine Academy is the only one permitted to display a battle flag, and for good reason. It is able to display this special flag because many Kings Point students were involved in several naval battles during World War II. The transport ships the students were serving on at the time frequently came under enemy attack. And when attacked, the crews of these ships and the students they carried fought back! Ultimately, 142 Kings Point students lost their lives in battle on the open seas during this tumultuous time. The Kings Point battle flag proudly displays the number 142 in their honor.

The Kings Point Experience

All new Kings Point students go through a two-week period of intensive training where they are introduced to Service Academy life and learn the customs and expectations of being a Service Academy student. After this introductory training period the first semester officially begins and the new students are then known as Midshipmen.

During students' sophomore and junior years at Kings Point, training transitions from the classroom to the sea. Midshipmen are assigned to merchant ships where they obtain valuable hands-on experience and even have the opportunity to visit many different countries. The senior year is spent back in the classroom where the academic theory and hands-on experience are combined, ensuring that all Midshipmen are fully prepared to enter a career at sea.

Like the other Service Academies, Kings Point admissions are competitive. In addition to a nomination by a U.S. congressman or senator, strong academic achievement is essential. All applicants must submit either SAT or ACT scores, submit an essay, obtain three letters of recommendation, pass a medical exam, and also pass a physical fitness exam. It may sound like a lot of hoops to jump through but it's definitely do-able.

All Midshipmen who graduate from Kings Point earn a bachelor of science in one of seven fields. Available majors include marine transportation, maritime operations and technology, logistics and intermodal transportation, marine engineering, marine engineering systems, and marine engineering and shipyard management. Students can also earn a hybrid degree in marine engineering and marine transportation.

Following graduation, Kings Point graduates must begin their service agreement. The service agreement requires all graduates to maintain a license as a Merchant Marine officer for a minimum of six years. Graduates are also required to apply to be an officer in the reserves of any branch of the U.S. Military. If the application is accepted (and why wouldn't it be?), graduates must fulfill the duties of a reserve officer for at least eight years. Finally, Kings Point graduates also have a five-year obligation to either work full time as an officer on a U.S. Merchant Marine ship, ashore in the maritime industry, or in any branch of the U.S. military.

The U.S. Merchant Marine Academy not only offers a free education to all accepted students, it also offers opportunities for incredible adventures on the open seas and the ability to visit many different nations. The combination of a top-notch free education, adventure, and substantial postgraduate opportunities makes the U.S.

Merchant Marine Academy truly unique among higher education institutions.

The United States Military Academy

The United States Military Academy (www.usma.edu), also known as West Point, is tasked with the creation of new officers specifically for the U.S. Army. The academy is located in West Point, New York, on a 16,000 acre campus overlooking the Hudson River. The academy is 55 miles north of New York City and has approximately 4,500 students and a staff of 600. West Point does not charge tuition, room, or board to any accepted students. In addition, Cadets, as the academy's students are known, receive a modest stipend to cover living and personal expenses.

The First Engineering School in the United States

West Point was established in 1802, shortly after the American Revolutionary War. The academy initially offered a curriculum in artillery and engineering and served as the only engineering school in the United States until 1824.

West Point has a very special place in United States history. Except for the earliest conflicts in the nation's history, West Point graduates have participated in every major conflict the United States has engaged in. West Point itself has seen its share of conflict as well since it was the site of a Continental Army garrison during the Revolutionary War. Benedict Arnold, who was at one time commander of the fort at West Point, earned his fame as a traitor by unsuccessfully attempting to turn the fort over to the British. And during the Civil War hundreds of West Point graduates became officers for both the Union and

Confederate armies. Many of the Cadets who resigned from the academy to fight on the side of their home states in the south were often reluctant to leave West Point since it was the most prestigious institute of its kind at the time. Graduating from West Point during that era virtually guaranteed a bright future and a promising career.

Many famous military leaders throughout U.S. history have been West Point graduates including George Armstrong Custer (who graduated last in his class), Jefferson Davis, Stonewall Jackson, John Pershing, Henry "Hap" Arnold, George S. Patton, Omar Bradley, and many others. Other notable alumni include more than a dozen astronauts, many Rhodes Scholars, corporate CEOs, academic leaders, numerous Medal of Honor recipients, and two Presidents of the United States, Ulysses S. Grant, and Dwight D. Eisenhower. Due to West Point's substantial historical significance, much of the academy's campus has been designated a National Historic Landmark.

The West Point Experience

Although West Point originally offered training only in engineering and military studies, it has since increased its academic offerings to include the natural sciences, social sciences, and the humanities. All West Point Cadets earn a bachelor of science due to the emphasis on the sciences in the core curriculum. The instructors and professors at West Point consist of a mix of both officers and civilians.

All West Point Cadets undergo rigorous military training during their time at the academy including basic training, additional field training, and advanced specialized training. In addition, all Cadets must also participate in one of the many sports offered each semester. This participation is mandatory and is considered as much a part of Cadet development as the academic and military training components. All West Point Cadets are commissioned as second lieutenants in the U.S. Army upon graduation.

To be admitted to West Point, applicants must be no older than 23 years of age, be unmarried, and without children. Approximately 1,300 new cadets are admitted each year. In addition, no admitted Cadets may transfer in any previously earned college credits from other schools. Having previous college credit is not necessarily prohibited; the academy simply requires all new Cadets to complete the entire program of study from start to finish at West Point. After graduation, Cadets transition to life as Army officers and must serve a minimum of five years of active duty in the U.S. Army followed by three years of reserve duty.

Without a doubt, West Point ranks as one of the most prestigious institutions of higher learning in the United States. It has a long and distinguished history and is well known for the hard-working and well-rounded students it graduates. Unfairly or not, West Point graduates often have their resumes moved to the top of the applicant pool. Employers are aware of the dedication and self-determination needed to graduate from such a high-quality school. These are the kinds of people employers look for.

The United States Naval Academy

The United States Naval Academy (www.usna.edu), also known as Annapolis, is tasked with the creation of new officers for both the U.S. Navy and the U.S. Marine Corps. The 338-acre campus and naval base is located in Annapolis, Maryland, about a half-hour drive from either Washington, D.C., or Baltimore, Maryland. The academy has approximately 4,400 students and a staff of 600. Annapolis does not charge tuition, room, or board for any accepted students. In addition, Midshipmen, as the academy's students are known, receive a modest stipend to cover living and personal expenses.

A High-Tech Academy for a High-Tech Navy

The U.S. Naval Academy was established in 1845 on the location of a former U.S. Army fort to train new naval officers and also to contribute to the modernization of the U.S. Navy of the era. From the very beginning the Annapolis curriculum was designed to acclimate students to life at sea. In fact, in its earliest days Annapolis students actually spent more time at sea obtaining experience on ships than they did in the classroom. Things are very different today. Although traditional academics are now the primary focus, significant leadership and professional training in a variety of areas is also included in the curriculum. They are training future Navy and Marine officers, after all.

To qualify for admission to Annapolis, applicants must be no older than 23, unmarried, and without children. In addition to submitting an application and securing a nomination, candidates must also submit SAT or ACT scores, letters of recommendation, complete a test of physical fitness, and pass a medical physical exam. After graduation, Midshipmen are typically commissioned as junior officers in either the U.S. Navy or the U.S. Marine Corps where they must fulfill a minimum five-year service obligation in exchange for their education.

All Midshipmen graduate with a bachelor of science in one of 22 majors. Available majors include several engineering disciplines, foreign languages, the sciences, the humanities, social sciences, and information technology. And like West Point, athletics at Annapolis are not optional. They are considered an integral part of developing leadership abilities, team cooperation, and physical fitness. As such, all Midshipmen must participate each semester in one of the many athletic programs at either the varsity, intramural, or club sports level. Each summer all Midshipmen are required to participate in a four-week assignment on naval vessels where they obtain valuable experience learning naval operations and interacting with active Navy personnel.

Annapolis graduates are a highly accomplished bunch. In fact, more Naval Academy graduates have become astronauts (more than 50 and counting) than from any other school. The Naval Academy has also graduated dozens of Rhodes Scholars, Medal of Honor recipients, many leaders in government, academia, and industry, and one President of the United States, Jimmy Carter.

The U.S. Naval Academy is a first-rate institution of higher learning where future leaders are forged rather than created. If you are looking for a school that will truly challenge you in every way without burdening you financially, Annapolis is an excellent choice.

The United States Coast Guard Academy

The United States Coast Guard Academy (www.cga.edu) is tasked with the creation of new officers specifically for the U.S. Coast Guard. The campus is located in New London, Connecticut, 47 miles southeast of Hartford, on the Long Island Sound coast. The academy has approximately 1,000 students and is the smallest of the five U.S. Service Academies.

The Coast Guard Academy does not charge tuition, room, or board for any accepted students. In addition, Cadets, as the academy's students are known, receive a modest stipend to cover living and personal expenses. Upon graduation, Cadets are commissioned as junior officers in the U.S. Coast Guard and have a minimum service obligation of five years.

A U.S. Service Academy with a "Small College" Feel

The U.S. Coast Guard Academy traces its roots all the way back to 1876 when the School of Instruction was established to train officers for the Revenue Cutter Service of the era. The Revenue Cutter Service was the predecessor of today's Coast Guard and was established in 1790 as a maritime organization to police the coastal waters of the United States. In 1915 the Revenue Cutter Service was combined with the United States Life Saving Service (a coastal rescue organization) to form the U.S. Coast Guard.

Due primarily to the school's small size and its picturesque campus overlooking the New London Harbor, today's U.S. Coast Guard Academy more closely resembles a small college than a university, unlike the other Service Academies. One distinct advantage of attending such a small school is that classes are usually smaller with fewer students. Most of the academy's classes have no more than 20 students each.

One of the more interesting aspects of the U.S. Coast Guard Academy is that it has its own training vessel, a 295-foot sailboat known as the *Eagle*. Built in 1933 in Germany, the *Eagle* was originally a training vessel for the German Navy but was turned over to the United States after World War II as war reparations. The sailboat was transferred directly to the U.S. Coast Guard Academy, given a new name, and has been used extensively for Cadet training ever since.

All U.S. Coast Guard Academy Cadets earn a bachelor of science in one of eight available majors including civil, electrical, and mechanical engineering, naval architecture and marine engineering, marine and environmental sciences, operations research and computer analysis, government, and management. Regardless of their chosen major, all Cadets must complete a core curriculum in coursework that builds leadership ability with a strong foundation in the sciences, ethics, and leadership. An arrangement has also been made with nearby Connecticut College that lets Cadets take additional courses for elective credit, if they so desire.

The admissions process and requirements for the U.S. Coast Guard Academy are essentially the same as the other service academies with one important exception. The U.S. Coast Guard Academy does not require a nomination. All applicants are evaluated based on their previous grades, test scores, and extracurricular activities.

The U.S. Coast Guard Academy Experience

New Cadets report to the academy the summer before their first semester officially begins where they go through an introductory training program known as Swab Summer to acclimate them to Service Academy life. Cadets typically spend their summers focusing on specialized training while the semesters involve a mix of both academics and specialized training.

Each summer training session is unique. In their second summer of training, Cadets spend 10 weeks aboard U.S. Coast Guard vessels performing a variety of basic duties. During their third summer Cadets take a variety of specialized training courses and also spend some time training new Cadets. Finally, in their fourth summer, Cadets spend 10 weeks aboard U.S. Coast Guard vessels serving as junior officers.

Like the other Service Academies, physical fitness is also a top priority for the U.S. Coast Guard Academy. All Cadets must participate in a sports program each semester. It isn't optional. Thankfully, there are many challenging, fun physical education courses to choose from including golf, scuba diving, martial arts, swimming, and many others. The academy also offers more than 20 intercollegiate sports and a wide variety of club and intramural sports that Cadets can participate in as well.

Today's modern Coast Guard does far more than most people even realize. Every single day the Coast Guard is involved in saving lives at sea, conducting search and rescue operations, investigating maritime accidents, stopping drugs from reaching our shores, and many other exciting things that are vitally important to national security. And don't make the mistake of thinking that all Coast Guard jobs are limited to those at sea. There are many other opportunities available including jobs in aviation, intelligence, engineering, shore operations, public affairs, and many others. If you are looking for a truly exciting job where every day is an adventure, the Coast Guard is definitely where the action is. And if an action-packed career in the Coast Guard sounds like something you'd be interested in, why not go in as a graduate of the U.S. Coast Guard Academy? Why not go in serving as an officer with a debt-free degree from this highly respected school?

The United States Air Force Academy

The United States Air Force Academy (www.usafa.af.mil) is tasked with the creation of new officers for the U.S. Air Force. The 18,000 acre campus is located in Colorado Springs, Colorado, 70 miles south of Denver, and has approximately 4,500 students and a staff of 600. The U.S. Air Force Academy does not charge tuition, room, or board for any accepted students. In addition, all Cadets, as the academy's students are known, receive a modest stipend to cover living and personal expenses.

New Kid on the Block

The U.S. Air Force Academy is the youngest of the U.S. Service Academies and has only been in existence since 1954 when Congress approved funding for its construction. This was only eight years after the U.S. Air Force was established as an official branch of the military, separate and distinct from its origins in the U.S. Army.

During this time period the United States was engaged in a Cold War with the Soviet Union and the newly formed Air Force would have been the first to retaliate in the event of a nuclear attack. As a first line of defense, the Air Force experienced rapid growth and technological change and needed a constant influx of new officers to maintain air superiority. A new Service Academy specifically for the fledgling branch was necessary to support its unique mission and to train highly skilled officers for what would quickly become the most technologically advanced air force in the world.

The U.S. Air Force Academy Experience

Military training at the U.S. Air Force Academy continues throughout the four years that Cadets attend, both during the semesters and the summers. Cadets' first exposure to military training happens during the summer prior to the start of the first semester in what is known as Basic Cadet Training, where they are acclimated to Service Academy life and go through a demanding physical training regimen. The next summer is spent learning to fly gliders, parachuting, and studying military operations. Many different options exist for the remaining two summers and Cadets have a lot of freedom to pursue training programs that interest them. Cadets can even participate in training programs offered by other military branches.

All Air Force Academy Cadets earn a bachelor of science due the technical nature of the core curriculum, although emphasis is placed on leadership and ethics as well. Majors are available in the sciences, engineering, humanities, and interdisciplinary studies.

Like the other Service Academies, all U.S. Air Force Academy Cadets are required to participate in athletics each semester. Many different sports programs are offered at both the intercollegiate and intramural levels, in addition to a variety of physical fitness classes including swimming, boxing, wrestling, martial arts, exercise physiology, tennis, golf, basketball, and others.

Graduates of the U.S. Air Force Academy are typically commissioned as second lieutenants in the U.S. Air Force and have a minimum service obligation of five years. Certain jobs, such as pilot or navigator, require much longer service obligations. Like the other Service Academies (with the exception of the Coast Guard Academy), applicants to the U.S. Air Force Academy must secure a nomination, be no older than 23, unmarried, and without children. Applicants must also pass a physical fitness test as well as a medical physical exam.

The U.S. Air Force Academy, along with the other Service Academies, represents an incredible opportunity to earn a college degree without any financial obligation. In addition, students learn many new skills and gain highly valuable experience that students in other schools could only dream of. Where else can you go to school for free and have a career waiting for you when you graduate? Not only that, but all of the Service Academies, with the exception of King's Point, give students a small monthly stipend to pay for living and personal expenses while pursuing their education. When it comes to earning a college degree, the Service Academies are truly in a league of their own.

More Debt-Free Degree Strategies Coming Up

We've just covered 12 different schools in the United States that don't charge any tuition whatsoever for any students who are accepted. And several of them don't charge room or board, either. But let's face it...these schools aren't a perfect fit for everybody. And not only that, but they don't accept an unlimited number of new students each year, either. Because of the incredible financial deal these schools represent and the limited number of new students who are accepted, competition for admission is strong.

If the tuition-free schools aren't right for you, does this mean you can't earn a college degree without accumulating a mountain of debt? Not at all. In the next two chapters we'll take a look at a strategy that lets you completely skip many of your lower-division courses by testing out of them. These challenge exams for college credit are accepted by nearly 3,000 colleges and universities and you can use them to skip one or more years of college courses and shorten your path to graduation. But perhaps the best thing about them is the tremendous savings they represent over tuition. Would you believe you can earn up to 30 credit hours of challenge exam credits for under $1,000? Did you know there are many schools that will let you test out of the first half of a bachelor's degree and earn a four-year degree in only two years? It's true. Let's see how it's done...

CHAPTER 6

Challenge It!

"He looks the whole world in the face for he owes not any man."

– Henry Wadsworth Longfellow

Repeat Offenders

Have you ever been in a situation where you already knew the material in a particular course but you were required to take it anyway? Maybe it was a requirement for your degree program or a necessary prerequisite before you could take a higher-level course. It can really be frustrating to have to sit through a course on something you already know, especially when you have to pay expensive tuition to do so. It can seem so redundant and like such a time-waster.

In most cases the courses that qualify as "repeat offenders" are the introductory courses that are required in the first two years of college. We're talking about such courses as intro to psychology, intro to sociology, history, natural sciences, and others. We've already talked in a previous chapter about how many of the courses you take in high school are essentially the same as what you cover in introductory college courses. Are you somehow "introduced" to a subject in a deeper and more meaningful way just because it's being taught in a college setting by a college professor? Although no two teachers or professors teach in exactly the same way, the answer is usually "no." By their very nature, introductory courses are not supposed to go very deep into a particular subject.

Wouldn't it be great if there was some way you could simply take some sort of final exam for introductory-level courses and move on? Good news…you can. Such exams do exist and they represent an incredible way to quickly knock out 30 or more credit hours of introductory courses while literally saving thousands of dollars in tuition at the same time. These challenge exams for college credit are accepted by nearly 3,000 colleges and universities. In fact, these days it's extremely rare to find a school that doesn't accept at least a few of them.

Save Time and Money

There are several unique benefits to obtaining college credit by taking (and passing) challenge exams. One of the most obvious benefits is the financial savings realized from skipping some of the introductory courses that make up the first two years of a college degree. How much money could you save by replacing 30 (or more) credit hours of introductory courses with a few inexpensive challenge exams? It's almost shocking. Be sure you're sitting down before we proceed.

Let's assume your school accepts 30 credit hours of challenge exam credit (not uncommon). Let's also assume your school charges $500 per credit hour for the same courses you are considering replacing with challenge exams ($500×30 credit hours = $15,000). Wow! That's a lot of money! Finally, let's assume that 30 credit hours of challenge exams comes to $1,000 (it's actually less, but we'll get to that).

By taking and passing $1,000 worth of challenge exams, you can save $14,000 in tuition that you otherwise would have had to spend to earn the exact same college credit by taking courses. Cha-ching! What's that sound? It's money in the bank, that's what. Do I have your attention yet?

Earning college credit with challenge exams is also a great way to decrease the time it takes to complete a college degree. This lets you shorten your path to either starting a career or beginning your grad school studies. These days it's not uncommon for many students to take five or even six years to complete a four-year degree. Why take any longer than you have to? For each additional year a person spends in school, one additional year of income from working will be lost in a lifetime. Time is money.

Yet another distinct advantage of earning college credit with challenge exams is that it doesn't matter where or how you obtained the knowledge. The exam doesn't care. It doesn't matter whether you acquired the knowledge from high school courses, from reading library books, or even from watching documentaries on TV. It truly doesn't matter.

If you are a history buff, for example, you may have no trouble passing a history exam with little or no studying. For those who work with computers on a regular basis, earning college credit for an introductory computer course by challenge exam may also be no problem. It's entirely possible to schedule and take several challenge exams in a day and walk out of the test center with three, six, or more college credits. Not bad for a day's work. And it's not as difficult as you may think. Thousands of people do it every year. I did it, and so can you!

Three Great Challenge Exams to Choose From

So, what are these great challenge exams? How do you take them? How do you get college credit for them? As it turns out, there are several different organizations that offer challenge exams for college credit. This is a good thing since it gives you a greater variety of subject exams to choose from. Let's take a look at the three most common types.

The three most common challenge exams are DSST (DANTES Subject Standardized Tests), CLEP (College Level Examination Program), and AP (Advanced Placement). DSST exams were originally created by the United States Department of Defense as a way for military personnel to acquire college credit for nontraditional learning. The acronym DANTES stands for "Defense Activity for Nontraditional Education Support." Thankfully, you no longer have to be on active duty in the military to be able to take these exams. They are now available for both military personnel and civilians and are administered by Prometric. CLEP and AP exams are by an organization known as the College Board. This is the same organization that's behind the infamous SAT exam.

Challenge exams have a lot more going for them than just the incredible financial savings they represent (as if that wasn't enough). For starters, most of them are in multiple-choice format. CLEP and DSST exams are multiple-choice while AP exams are in multiple-choice and short answer format. This lets you use the process of elimination (or take a wild guess) on questions you aren't 100 percent sure about. Unlike the SAT there is no penalty for selecting a wrong answer. And unlike earning a bad grade in (or failing) a traditional college course, if you don't earn a passing score on a particular challenge exam, no record of the attempt is made on your college transcript. This means you don't have to carry an "F" on your transcript from a failed attempt at a challenge exam like you would from a failed course. Nice! Finally, most schools do not award letter grades for credits earned by challenge exams. Instead, they simply record a "Pass" or "CR" (Credit) on your transcript. This means a score that barely passes is treated the same as one where every single question was answered correctly. Even if you barely squeak by on a challenge exam, it doesn't matter. You still get full credit for the course and your GPA is not adversely affected.

It's very easy to schedule and take CLEP and DSST exams. AP exams, however, are a different story (more on that later). CLEP and DSST exams are typically administered at test centers in community colleges, four-year colleges, and universities while AP exams are typically administered in high schools. Test center locations are very common so unless you live in a very remote location, you should not have to drive far to get to one. Finding a test center is also very easy since both CLEP and DSST list all test center locations on their web sites. Once you have selected the exams you wish to take, simply call the school and ask to speak to the CLEP or DSST exam administrator. You'll need to make an appointment to take an exam, so expect to schedule a date one to two weeks out. You can schedule to take one challenge exam or several at a time…it's entirely up to you. Also, be aware that some test centers may charge a small fee for their services above the fees for the exams. Some do and some don't.

Obtaining college credit for taking and passing challenge exams is very straightforward. Before scheduling to take any exam though, be sure to check your school's challenge exam policy to see which exams they accept for college credit. This information is usually found on a school's web site or in its academic policies. After you have taken and passed one or more challenge exams, you simply order an official transcript from the organization that oversees the exams and have it sent to your school. It's just as simple as that. The process is essentially the same as transferring college credit from one school to another. It's a good idea to complete all of the exams you intend to take before ordering a transcript since there is a small transcript fee involved.

Another thing to keep in mind is the amount of credit awarded for a passing score on each challenge exam varies from school to school. Also, what qualifies as a passing score varies from school to school as well. And of course, some schools will permit more exam credit than others to be applied toward a degree. Most major state universities will accept around 30 credit hours of challenge exam credit while others, such as Liberty University, Troy University, the University of Wyoming, and others will allow you to complete the first half of a bachelor's degree entirely with challenge exam credit. Imagine the savings!

CLEP EXAMS

The multiple-choice CLEP exams (http://clep.collegeboard.org) are administered by computer in a test center and are $77 each. The range of possible scores for any CLEP exam is between 20 and 80 and the most common passing score is a 50. It's important to keep in mind, however, that some schools may require a higher score before they will award college credit in certain subjects. With the exception of the English Composition exam, which has an essay component that requires special grading, all CLEP exam grading is automated and grades are reported the same day you take the exams. The following is a list of CLEP exams and the number of college credits that are typically awarded for passing scores.

American Government	(3)
American Literature	(6)
Analyzing and Interpreting Literature	(6)
Biology	(6)
Calculus	(3)
Chemistry	(6)
College Algebra	(3)
College Mathematics	(6)
English Composition	(6)
English Literature	(6)
Financial Accounting	(3)
French Language (Levels 1 and 2)	(6 – 12)
Freshman College Composition	(6)
German Language (Levels 1 and 2)	(6 – 12)
History of the United States I: Early Colonization to 1877	(3)
History of the United States II: 1865 to the Present	(3)
Human Growth and Development	(3)
Humanities	(6)
Information Systems and Computer Applications	(3)
Introduction to Educational Psychology	(3)
Introductory Business Law	(3)
Introductory Psychology	(3)
Introductory Sociology	(3)
Natural Sciences	(6)
Pre-Calculus	(3)

Principles of Macroeconomics	(3)
Principles of Management	(3)
Principles of Marketing	(3)
Principles of Microeconomics	(3)
Social Sciences and History	(6)
Spanish Language (Levels 1 and 2)	(6 – 12)
Western Civilization I: Ancient Near East to 1648	(3)
Western Civilization II: 1648 to the Present	(3)

DSST EXAMS

Unlike CLEP exams, which are administered on a computer, the multiple-choice DSST exams (www.getcollegecredit.com) are administered in old-fashioned pencil and paper format. The answer sheets are the "fill in the bubble" forms we're all familiar with that are automatically graded by Scantron machines. The range of possible scores for any DSST exam is between 200 and 500 and the most common passing score is a 400. DSST scores are also reported differently than CLEP exams where grades are reported the same day you take the exams. Scores for DSST exams are reported by mail within three to four weeks of exam completion. DSST exams are $80 each.

As you look over the list of available DSST exams, you'll notice that some of them have titles that are very similar to a few of the CLEP exams. Be careful not to take a CLEP exam and a DSST exam on the same subject. Schools consider this overlap and usually won't award any additional credit. The following is a list of DSST exams and the number of college credits that are typically awarded for passing scores in addition to whether they are for lower-division (L) credit or upper division (U). While all of the CLEP exams are for lower-division credit, some of the DSST exams give you the opportunity to test out of upper-division courses.

Art of the Western World	(3/L)
Astronomy	(3/L)
Business Ethics and Society	(3/U)
Business Law II	(3/U)
Business Mathematics	(3/L)
Civil War and Reconstruction	(3/U)
Criminal Justice	(3/U)
Environment and Humanity	(3/L)
Ethics in America	(3/U)
Fundamentals of College Algebra	(3/L)
Fundamentals of Counseling	(3/L)
Foundations of Education	(3/L)
General Anthropology	(3/L)
Here's to Your Health	(3/U)
History of the Vietnam War	(3/L)
Human/Cultural Geography	(3/L)
Human Resource Management	(3/L)
Introduction to Business	(3/L)
Introduction to Computing	(3/L)
Introduction to Law Enforcement	(3/L)
Introduction to the Modern Middle East	(3/L)
Introduction to World Religions	(3/U)
Life-Span Developmental Psychology	(3/L)

Management Information Systems	(3/U)
Money and Banking	(3/U)
Organizational Behavior	(3/L)
Personal Finance	(3/L)
Physical Geology	(3/L)
Principles of Statistics	(3/L)
Principles of Physical Science I	(3/L)
Principles of Finance	(3/U)
Principles of Financial Accounting	(3/L)
Principles of Public Speaking	(3/L)
Principles of Supervision	(3/L)
Rise and Fall of the Soviet Union	(3/U)
Substance Abuse	(3/U)
Technical Writing	(3/L)
Western Europe since 1945	(3/L)

AP Exams

AP Exams (Advanced Placement) are best suited for those who are still in high school since the exams are designed to be taken at the end of year-long high school courses. Students typically enroll in high school courses in subjects that have been designated "AP courses" and then take the corresponding AP exams at the end of the school year. AP exams are only administered once per year in May. In contrast, CLEP and DSST exams can be taken any time of the year. There is an $86 fee for each AP exam. www.collegeboard.com/student/testing/ap/about.html

AP exams are a little different from the multiple-choice CLEP and DSST exams. AP exams are a combination of multiple-choice, problem solving, or short essay. And there is one lone AP exam, AP Studio Art, that is substantially different from the others. In AP Studio Art students submit portfolios of completed art for review.

AP exams are scored on a scale of one to five with a three being the most common passing score. There are some schools, however, that require scores of four or even five for college credit to be awarded in certain subjects. Just like CLEP and DSST, no two schools will have the exact same AP policy. After completing one or more AP exams, a transcript of your score(s) can then be ordered and sent to the school of your choice to be added to your official transcript.

Although AP exams were designed to be taken at the end of a high school AP course, it's important to point out that you do not have to be a high school student to take any of these exams, nor do you have to be enrolled in a high school AP course. In fact, there are many home-schooled students and even adults who take AP exams. If you aren't a high school student and would like to take an AP exam, you will need to contact AP Services by March 1 to find out where and when the exams will be administered in your community:

AP Services
PO Box 6671
Princeton, NJ 08541-6671
Phone: (609) 771-7300 or (888) 225-5427

The following is a list of available AP exams and the number of college credits that is typically awarded for passing scores. As you'll quickly notice, many of these exams have a range of possible credits such as (3-6) or (4-8). There's a simple explanation for this. Many schools will award credit for one course for a passing score of a three or four and credit for two courses for a higher score of four or five. Whenever credit for two courses is awarded for passing one exam, it's typically for two courses that are designed to be taken in sequence, such as Biology 101 and Biology 102.

Art History	(6)
Biology	(4-8)
Calculus AB	(3-6)
Calculus BC	(3-6)
Chemistry	(4-8)
Chinese Language and Culture	(3-6)
Comparative Government and Politics	(3)
Computer Science A	(3)
English Language & Composition	(3-6)
English Literature & Composition	(3-6)
Environmental Science	(4-8)
European History	(3-6)
French Language	(3-6)
German Language	(3-6)
Human Geography	(3)
Japanese Language and Culture	(3-6)
Latin: Vergil	(3-6)
Macroeconomics	(3)
Microeconomics	(3)
Music Theory	(3-6)
U.S. Government and Politics	(3)
Physics B	(4-8)
Physics C	(4)

Psychology	(3)
Spanish Language	(3-6)
Spanish Literature	(3-6)
Statistics	(3-6)
Studio Art	(3)
U.S. History	(3-6)
World History	(3-6)

If you are not a high school student, AP exams are probably not the best challenge exams to use as part of your affordable degree strategy. The main problem with AP exams for adult students is that they are only offered once per year. CLEP and DSST exams are offered year-round at test centers all across the nation. If a satisfactory score is not obtained on a CLEP or DSST exam, you only have to wait six months before taking a failed exam again. This is not the case with AP exams. You have to wait one calendar year to retake a failed AP exam. If you do happen take an AP exam and don't earn a satisfactory score, however, it is still possible to take the corresponding CLEP or DSST exam and earn the college credit.

Challenge Exam Preparation

By now we've firmly established that challenge exams represent an amazing way to save big on tuition and to decrease the time it takes to graduate. But what is the best way to prepare for these exams? Is it really necessary to read all the way through a 1,000 page textbook on psychology to pass the Intro to Psychology CLEP exam? Thankfully, no. Many different study guides have been written for these exams that were designed to get you up to speed on the material in the least amount of time possible. Your local bookstore probably already has a great selection to choose from. And don't forget to look for bargains online as well.

CLEP, DSST, and AP exam study guides are designed to fully prepare you to take and pass the exams. They are not designed to teach you everything there is to know about the subjects they cover. This is a good thing since the exam prep guides let you focus in on the material that matters on the exams and ignore the material that doesn't. If you are already familiar with a particular subject, you may only need a week or two to review a study guide before taking the exam. And even if you are nearing the end of a year-long AP course, it's still a good idea to pick up and review an AP study guide on the exam(s) you plan on taking.

Is it possible to pass a challenge exam with little or no studying? Yes, it happens all the time. This is especially true for subjects you are already very familiar with. There are also some truly ambitious people who have the ability to pick up a study guide, cram for one or two weeks and then pass the exam with no prior knowledge of the subject. Remember, these exams were designed to measure college-level knowledge of specific subjects. It doesn't matter how or where you acquired the knowledge…or even if it only takes you one week to do so. The exam doesn't care.

Without a doubt, CLEP, DSST, and AP exams represent one of the best ways to slash your college tuition bills and to substantially decrease the time it takes to graduate there is. These exams should be used as a first-line strategy in any affordable college degree plan.

Even More Challenge Exams Coming Up

Did you think we were finished with challenge exams for college credit? Not at all. So far we've only covered the three most popular types of these exams. There are others available that are definitely worth exploring. Many of these exams are in subjects that are not covered by CLEP/DSST/AP exams and some of them are even available for upper-level credit. In the next chapter we'll take an in-depth look at these exams and how you can incorporate them into your degree plan.

CHAPTER 7

Do You Accept the Challenge?

"Education is what remains when one has forgotten everything he learned in school."

– Albert Einstein

CLEP, DSST, and AP exams are widely recognized and inexpensive. As such, they should be the foundation of your affordable college degree plan. There are, however, other less-common challenge exams that are worth exploring. Although these exams are not as well known as the three we discussed in the previous chapter, they do offer exams for many courses that CLEP, DSST, and AP don't cover. In addition, some of them are for upper-level credit, giving you a way to take challenge exams in place of courses for your major, minor, or to fulfill upper-level electives.

One of the disadvantages of these lesser-known exams is that not all schools have guidelines established for accepting them. In fact, some school officials may not even be aware that these exams even exist. If you are interested in taking one or more of these exams for college credit and your school doesn't have guidelines established for them, all is not lost. You can still petition your school to accept them.

Petitioning your school to accept an unfamiliar challenge exam is really not the daunting task it may at first seem. The first step is to meet with your academic adviser and let him know that you would like to use one or more of these challenge exams in place of traditional courses. Your academic adviser will know the steps to take that are specific to your school for having them approved. It's a good idea to be prepared to tell your adviser a little about the exams you are interested in and the school or organization that's behind them. In other words, you may have to "educate the educators" about them since they are not as well known as CLEP, DSST, and AP. There is, of course, no guarantee that your school will approve any of these challenge exams…but it never hurts to ask, right?

Excelsior College Exams (ECE)

Excelsior College (www.excelsior.edu) is a nonprofit college in Albany, New York, that offers nearly 50 challenge exams for college credit that are accepted at over 900 colleges and universities. These exams are probably the most well known of the three types of exams we'll look at in this chapter. ECE exams are offered in the subjects of nursing, education, business, humanities, and the sciences, many of which are for upper-level credit. The exams are computer-based and are administered by Pearson VUE at test centers in 165 countries (www.vue.com). ECE exams may be in either multiple-choice format, essay format, or mixed (multiple-choice and short essay), depending on which ones you are taking.

Excelsior College's nursing challenge exams, in particular, are very popular and for good reason. Excelsior College's nursing school is the largest in the United States. To give its students more options to earn college credit, the college's nursing school created a variety of affordable nursing challenge exams, some of which are worth up to eight credit hours each. ECE nursing challenge exams are also very popular with nursing students in other schools and are now commonly accepted by nursing schools all across the nation.

Although Excelsior College is a comprehensive liberal arts college that offers many degree programs of its own, you do not have to be enrolled in an Excelsior College degree program to take ECE exams. They are open to anyone who would like to take them. After passing all of the ECE exams you intend to take, you can simply order a transcript and have it sent to the school of your choice to use as transfer credit.

Registering to take ECE exams is a very simple and straightforward process. It's all done online. The first step is to create a user account on Excelsior College's web site. After your user account is established, you can then schedule one or more ECE exams at a Pearson VUE test center of your choice. Be prepared to pay for the exams during the registration process with a major credit card. Although it's possible to reschedule an exam, it's important to keep in mind that all ECE exams must be taken within six months of registration.

ECE Exam Prep

If you are interested in taking one or more ECE exams, there are several study resources available. For starters, Excelsior College provides free outlines of each exam that can be downloaded from its web site. You can then purchase the recommended textbook (used, of course) and then recoup most of your investment by reselling it online after completing the exam.

Instantcert Academy (www.instantcert.com) is another valuable resource you can use to prepare for ECE exams (as well as CLEP, DSST, and TECEP exams). Instantcert Academy is a subscription-based online study tool that helps you to quickly prepare for these exams with its interactive software. The $20 per month subscription gives you access to all available exam study materials and can be canceled at any time.

Don't forget EBay! EBay is a great resource for finding affordable ECE exam study materials. This is such a great resource because there are so many people who purchase exam study guides, pass their exams, and then sell the study guides online to recoup their investments. Definitely take advantage of these used study materials for big savings. A simple search for "Excelsior College" on EBay almost always turns up many different study guides for sale.

One of the most valuable resources you can ever use to prepare for any exam is a good study buddy. Thankfully, finding others who are preparing for the same ECE exams you are is just a mouse click away at the EC Study Group (www.ecstudygroup.com). The EC Study Group is a discussion forum just for students who are preparing to take ECE exams and can be a valuable asset if you ever need to ask a specific question about a particular exam. Although the online community mainly focuses on ECE nursing exams, the school's other exams are covered as well. As an added bonus, you can take advantage of the section of the forum where used ECE study materials are listed for sale to grab some bargains.

The ECE Exams

The following is a list of available ECE exams and the number of credits that Excelsior College awards for passing scores. Each exam is also designated as either lower-level (L) or upper-level (U), based on how Excelsior College awards credit. Also included is the price for each exam. The per-credit-hour fee for the various exams is not consistent. The Fundamentals of Nursing exam, for example, offers eight credit hours for only $330 ($41.25 per credit hour) while many other three-credit-hour exams are offered for as little as $95 each ($31.67 per credit hour).

ECE Arts And Sciences Exams:

Abnormal Psychology	(3/U)	$305
Anatomy and Physiology	(6/L)	$415
Bioethics: Philosophical Issues	(3/U)	$305
Cultural Diversity	(3/U)	$305
Earth Science	(3/L)	$305
English Composition	(6/L)	$415
Ethics: Theory and Practice	(3/U)	$305
Foundations of Gerontology	(3/U)	$305
Interpersonal Communication	(3/L)	$305
Introduction to Music	(3/L)	$305
Introduction to Philosophy	(3/L)	$305
Juvenile Delinquency	(3/U)	$305
Life Span Developmental Psychology	(3/L)	$305
Microbiology	(3/L)	$305
Pathophysiology	(3/U)	$95

Psychology of Adulthood and Aging	(3/U)	$95
Research Methods in Psychology	(3/U)	$95
Social Psychology	(3/U)	$95
World Conflicts Since 1900	(3/U)	$305
World Population	(3/L)	$95

ECE Business Exams:

Business Law	(3/L)	$95
Financial Accounting	(3/L)	$95
Human Resource Management	(3/U)	$95
Labor Relations	(3/U)	$95
Managerial Accounting	(3/L)	$95
Macroeconomics	(3/L)	$95
Microeconomics	(3/L)	$95
Organizational Behavior	(3/U)	$95
Principles of Management	(3/L)	$95
Principles of Marketing	(3/L)	$95
Workplace Communication with Computers	(3/L)	$95

ECE Education Exam:

Literacy Instruction in the Elementary School	(6/U)	$415

ECE Nursing Exams (Lower-Level):

Essentials of Nursing Care: Chronicity	(3/L)	$305
Essentials of Nursing Care: Health Differences	(3/L)	$305
Essentials of Nursing Care: Health Safety	(3/L)	$305
Essentials of Nursing Care: Reproductive Health	(3/L)	$305
Fundamentals of Nursing	(8/L)	$330
Health Differences Across the Life Span 1	(3/L)	$305
Health Differences Across the Life Span 2	(3/L)	$305
Health Differences Across the Life Span 3	(3/L)	$305
Maternal and Child Nursing	(6/L)	$330
Transition to the Registered Professional Nurse Role	(3/L)	$305

ECE Nursing Exams (Upper-Level):

Adult Nursing	(8/U)	$330
Community Focused Nursing	(4/U)	$330
Management in Nursing	(4/U)	$330
Maternal and Child Nursing	(8/U)	$330
Psychiatric/Mental Health Nursing	(8/U)	$330
Research in Nursing	(3/U)	$305

No question about it...ECE exams are an incredible deal, especially for upper-level credit. While the cost per exam varies depending on which exam you are taking, the per-credit-hour cost for all of the exams falls within the average range for community college tuition (or less). If your school accepts ECE exams for credit, don't overlook this incredible opportunity to earn college credit for much less than you would pay for tuition and in potentially less time than by taking courses in the same subjects.

Thomas Edison State College Examination Program (TECEP)

Thomas Edison State College (www.tesc.edu), one of New Jersey's 12 state colleges, offers 20 challenge exams that can be taken for college credit. The pencil-and-paper TECEP exams are primarily multiple-choice with some containing short-answer questions. These exams are a real bargain at only $99 each.

Like CLEP, DSST, and AP, credit for a passing TECEP score is typically recorded as a "Pass" or "CR" on transcripts without a letter grade. And like Excelsior College, you do not need to be enrolled in a degree program with Thomas Edison State College to take one or more of these exams. They are great to use as transfer credit for another school.

TECEP exams have a couple of interesting things going for them that make them very compelling. First, you've probably already noticed some degree of overlap in the various CLEP, DSST, and AP exams. In other words, a few of the same exams are offered by each of these three organizations although they might have slightly different titles. Most of the TECEP exams, however, are for courses that aren't already covered by other exams. They are unique. And not only that, but some of them are worth upper-level credit as well.

Another advantage of TECEP is you don't have to travel to a test center to take these exams. They can be taken locally, right in your own community and are administered by a local proctor. A proctor is someone in your community who watches you take an exam to ensure no cheating takes place. The exam is typically sent directly to the proctor who administers it and then sends the completed exam back to the school to be graded. The only time you will have any contact with the exam is during the time you are actually taking it. Suitable proctors usually include local college officials, public librarians, or others as designated by the school.

The following is a list of available TECEP exams and the amount of credit that is typically awarded for passing scores. In addition, each exam is designated as either lower-level (L) or upper-level (U) based on the type of credit Thomas Edison State College awards.

Exam	Credit/Level
Advertising	(3/U)
Business in Society	(3/U)
English Composition I	(3/L)
English Composition II	(3/L)
Federal Income Taxation	(3/U)
Financial Institutions and Markets	(3/U)
Introduction to Human Services	(3/L)
Introduction to News Reporting	(3/L)
Introduction to Political Science	(3/L)
Marketing Communications	(3/U)
Marriage and the Family	(3/L)

Network Technology	(3/U)
Operations Management	(3/U)
Public Relations Thought and Practice	(3/L)
Psychology of Women	(3/L)
Sales Management	(3/U)
Strategic Management	(3/U)
The Science of Nutrition	(3/L)
Security Analysis and Portfolio Management	(3/U)
Technical Writing	(3/L)

For each TECEP exam, Thomas Edison State College provides a free test description that can be downloaded and reviewed before you even register. Each test description provides an outline of the content you will see on the exam and recommend textbooks to review. Some even include sample questions that let you get an idea of how difficult the questions will be.

UExcel Exams

UExcel exams (www.uexceltest.com) are the new kid on the block when it comes to challenge exams for college credit. First offered in 2009, these exams were developed as a joint venture between Excelsior College and the international media company, Pearson. It's important to point out that these exams were not created just for Excelsior College students. They were developed to be used by students in schools all across the nation and around the world.

UExcel Exams have received a nod of approval from a very important player in the world of higher education. The American Council on Education (ACE) has evaluated

UExcel exams and has recommended college credit for them. We'll get into the importance of being ACE evaluated in the next chapter. But for now you can rest assured that this is a good thing…a very, very good thing.

Why would you want to consider UExcel exams instead of CLEP, DSST, or AP exams? After all, UExcel offers the same exams the others offer. So what's so special about them? The one thing that makes these exams so compelling is all of the credit you earn from taking and passing these exams is recorded with a letter grade directly on an Excelsior College transcript. When you have finished taking all of the UExcel exams you plan on taking, you can then have an official Excelsior College transcript sent to the school of your choice as transfer credit, with no transcript fee.

There are currently eight UExcel exams available although more are being developed. The available exams and the number of credits recommended for passing scores are:

MAT150 Calculus	(4)
ENG110 College Writing	(3)
PSY101 Introduction to Psychology	(3)
SOC105 Introduction to Sociology	(3)
PHY140 Physics	(6)
POL170 Political Science	(3)
SPA102 Spanish Language	(6)
MAT210 Statistics	(3)

UExcel exams can be taken at any of the Pearson VUE test centers in 165 countries (www.vue.com). The exams are administered on computers and cost $95 each. The exam format is multiple-choice and fill in the blank.

UExcel has excellent content guides available for each exam that can be download from its web site. These content guides are valuable road maps, showing you exactly what you need to focus on to succeed. They also include practice questions and lists of recommended resources to help you efficiently prepare to take the exams.

UExcel exams can be an excellent addition to your affordable college degree plan, as long as your school will accept them for credit. As with any challenge exam, don't make any assumptions. Be absolutely certain your school will accept all of the challenge exams you are interested in before you even register to take them. Since UExcel exams have been ACE evaluated and they are recorded on official Excelsior College transcripts, there's a good chance your school will accept them. You'll never know unless you ask.

Aside from attending a school that doesn't charge any tuition or earning college credit from your local community college, challenge exams for college credit represent one of the most affordable ways to earn college credit. But the incredible savings aren't the only benefit. Why not throw some challenge exam credit into your degree plan and finish your four-year degree in only three years? Or better yet, why not attend a college or university that accepts up to 60 credit hours of challenge exam credit? You can amaze your friends, family, and coworkers by telling them you earned your four-year degree in only two years. They'll think you're a genius. And in fact, you will be a genius…a financial genius for all the money you saved.

CHAPTER 8

Ace It!

"Debt is like any other trap, easy enough to get into, but hard enough to get out of."

- Henry Wheeler Shaw

It's a Trap!

Have you ever seen one of those advertisements that offer college degrees for life experience? You know, the ones that claim they can award a college degree based on nothing more than an evaluation of your resume and your previous life experiences? They usually offer to evaluate your resume for a college degree for "only" a few hundred or perhaps a few thousand dollars. Sounds like an incredible deal, right? And not only that but they usually claim to be properly accredited. Advertisements for "life experience" degrees are found in many different places including various magazines, web sites, and they can even show up in online search results for education-related search queries.

The next time you encounter one of these advertisements, skip over it just as fast as you can. Don't even look back. It's a trap! The "universities" that offer such life experience degrees are known as "diploma mills" or "degree mills" and are usually nothing more than scam operations. The perpetrators of the fraud don't care at all about your educational background or experiences. They're only interested in your money. The only thing you'll get by answering one of these advertisements (other than a substantial charge on your credit card statement) is a diploma in the mail that is just as useless as the paper it's printed on. Oh, and the organizations these "universities" claim accreditation from are usually fictitious entities of their own creation.

Unfortunately, each year many people fall victim to these scams and end up losing their careers once it's discovered that the "degrees" they used to get their jobs or earn promotions are completely fake. When this happens it can leave a big black stain on a person's resume (from being fired) and can make finding future employment difficult when potential employers call previous employers or do background checks. Many people don't realize they are falling for a scam when responding to advertisements for life experience degrees, while others know fully what they are doing but do it anyway, hoping their little secret will never be discovered. If you have ever been tempted to answer one of these advertisements but your "spidey sense" was telling you something seemed fishy, give yourself a pat on the back. Your intuition was right.

While the life experience degree is something you should definitely avoid, there is an interesting alternative that's definitely worth considering. Did you know it's possible to turn many previous learning experiences into college credit that you can use to earn a college degree through legitimate, properly accredited colleges and universities? It's true. You can receive college credit for the completion of many corporate training courses, military training programs, training for volunteer organizations, and many other learning experiences that did not occur within the walls of a college or university. You can earn college credit for the vegetable garden you grow each year (horticulture), for becoming a certified aerobics instructor (physical education), for all of the amazing pictures of the galaxy you've captured through your telescope (astronomy), and for many other activities and pursuits you've explored in your life.

There are two methods for acquiring legitimate college credit for these previous learning experiences. The first is through a method known as portfolio assessment and the second is through an organization known as the American Counsel on Education.

Portfolio Assessment

Portfolio assessment is a strategy you can use to earn college credit for many previous learning experiences that occurred outside of the traditional academic setting and is offered by many schools all across the nation. Be careful though…don't confuse portfolio assessment with the fraudulent "life experience" degrees that are sold to many unsuspecting victims. There is a *big* difference. Some schools may refer to portfolio assessment as prior learning assessment or experiential learning but they all refer to the same thing.

The portfolio assessment concept is simple. If you have already acquired college-level knowledge in a particular course offered by your school, you can submit a "portfolio" of documentation, photographs, or anything else that proves you know the material and earn college credit for the course. With portfolio assessment it doesn't matter how you learned the material. You could have obtained knowledge on a particular subject from watching PBS documentaries, reading how-to books, or through on-the-job training. With portfolio assessment the method you used to learn a particular subject is irrelevant. It's what you know that's important. After submitting a portfolio for a particular subject, it will be evaluated by someone who teaches the subject you are challenging. If the evaluator approves of the material you submit in your portfolio, you receive credit for the course.

What subjects can you earn college credit in through portfolio assessment? Just about anything, really. It could be in any traditional subject offered by your school such as photography, foreign languages, computers, art, or anything else that you have acquired evidence or documentation of college-level learning. Are you a green belt in a martial art? Why not turn it into physical education credit? Do you love to write poetry or short stories? Sounds like creative writing credit to me. You are only limited by your school's policy on this type of credit. Most schools do impose a limit on how many portfolio assessment credits you can use toward your degree, so be sure to review your school's policy before putting together your first portfolio.

Portfolio assessment is an ideal way to turn a hobby into college credit. Are you passionate about photography? Do you enjoy taking pictures of birds, flowers, landscapes, and other things in nature? Why not put together a portfolio of your best photos and earn college credit in nature photography? Do you enjoy playing a musical instrument? Perhaps you even write your own songs. Why not put together a portfolio where you demonstrate your musical skills in front of an evaluator and earn college credit in performing arts? You could submit another portfolio consisting of songs you have written and earn college credit in music composition (or music appreciation). Do you enjoy researching your family tree? Why not submit a portfolio consisting of all of the family documents you've unearthed and the family tree you've mapped out and earn college credit in genealogy? As you can see, there are many different hobbies that can easily be turned into college credit.

So, what kind of things are included in a typical portfolio? The short answer is...it depends. A successful portfolio could consist of nothing more than a certificate of completion or a professional certification in something. There are many things that are taught by various community organizations that are also taught by colleges and universities for college credit. Just a few examples include basic first aid, CPR, personal finance, health and wellness programs, various workforce development programs, and many others. If you completed a course in personal training from an organization in your community, what sense does it make to take the course again in college just to earn college credit? It doesn't make any sense. Portfolio assessment lets you submit a professional certification in personal training as evidence of course completion, obtain the college credit, and move on to something else.

Portfolio assessment can be used to turn many different licenses and certifications into college credit. A few examples include volunteer training certifications, a private pilot's license, Microsoft, Cisco, and other computer certifications, and many others. The process for obtaining college credit through portfolio assessment is pretty much the same from school to school with only minor variations. Many schools even offer courses or seminars that give you an overview of the process and show you how to put together a successful portfolio.

One thing you should be aware of if you are considering portfolio assessment is that you can only use this method to obtain college credit for courses offered by the school you are enrolled in. For example, if you're a pro at taking out the garbage and want to use portfolio assessment to earn college credit in The Joy of Garbage (as offered by Santa Clara University) but your school doesn't offer the course, you're just out of luck.

To use the portfolio assessment method, you must first go through your school's course catalog and pick out the courses you believe you have already acquired college-level knowledge in. You have to be able to demonstrate that you have acquired college-level knowledge for the entire course…no partial credit will be awarded. Once you have picked out the courses you want to go for, you then assemble a portfolio of evidence for each individual course you are pursuing with this method. Examples of evidence include live performances, professional certifications, certificates of completion, tasks you have completed at work, paintings you've completed, short stories, novels and poetry you've written, and others. Evidence can be just about anything that proves you have learned the material and deserve college credit for a particular course.

When assembling a portfolio, it's important not to make the mistake of merely documenting the amount of time you spent doing something as evidence of knowledge. Remember, this is not about "life experience." If a portfolio consists of little more than a resume listing the years you spent engaged in a particular activity, you are unlikely to earn college credit for the portfolio. You may have hundreds of hours of experience programming in Java, for example, but if you don't have anything to show for it, you can't obtain credit in Java programming through portfolio assessment. It's all about the evidence. As they say in Missouri, "show me." Fill your Java Language portfolio with examples of Java programs you have written. "Wow" them with your best work.

Although portfolio assessment may at first sound like a complex process, it's really not. Definitely take advantage of any seminars your school offers for earning college credit with this method. If you are still unsure of whether this is something you want to attempt, try portfolio assessment for just one course to help you better understand the process. You can always submit more portfolios for evaluation after you've completed the first one to get a feel for the process.

The cost of portfolio assessment varies from school to school. Some schools charge the same tuition per credit hour for portfolio assessment as they do for regular courses. Others charge much less. Whether this option will save you money depends entirely upon the school you are attending. If you find that your school doesn't charge less for portfolio assessment, you can still come out ahead by saving time. Portfolio assessment makes it possible to take fewer courses to graduate so you can earn your degree more quickly and enter the workforce sooner. Time is money.

Portfolio assessment is yet another arrow in your quiver you can use to shorten your path to a college degree and possibly save money in the process. Don't let the task of assembling and submitting evidence of learning scare you away from using this great strategy.

The American Counsel on Education (ACE)

The American Counsel on Education (ACE) (www.acenet.edu/nationalguide) is an organization in the United States made up of nearly 2,000 colleges, universities, and other education-affiliated institutions. It was established in 1918 for the purpose of conducting research on the continuous improvement of higher education and is most well known for the creation of the

General Education Diploma (GED) examination program, which it continues to oversee. ACE also offers a unique training program known as the ACE Fellows Program, which is a special training program for academics who intend to pursue an administrative position at a college or university. The program is designed to prepare academics for such leadership positions as department chair, dean, and even chancellor, or president. As you can see, ACE is a pretty big deal in the world of higher education.

ACE has also created a highly valuable program for college students that, sadly, few people even know about. It's time to change that. Through this program it's possible for many students to eliminate one or more years of coursework and save many thousands of dollars on tuition. Through its College Credit Recommendation Service, ACE has taken on the tedious job of evaluating literally hundreds of training programs from many different companies and organizations.

The way the College Credit Recommendation Service works is simple. After conducting a thorough evaluation of a particular training program, ACE will make the recommendation that college credit be awarded for its completion if it was found to be comparable to a traditional college course in both content and rigor. Training programs that have been approved for college credit by ACE are usually referred to as "ACE evaluated." The ACE website contains a comprehensive list of all training programs that have been deemed worthy of college credit.

What does this mean for you as a student? If you have completed one or more corporate training programs or have completed training programs through volunteer or other organizations, there is a possibility that you may be able to turn that training into college credit and apply it to your degree program for the price of a transcript fee ($40). Not a bad deal, eh?

There are so many companies that have had their training programs evaluated by ACE that it simply isn't possible to include a comprehensive list in this chapter. However, the following is a brief sample to give you an idea of the types of companies and organizations ACE has evaluated:

- The American Payroll Association
- The United States Navy
- Curves International
- Delta Airlines
- The Federal Bureau of Investigation
- General Motors
- IBM
- McDonald's
- Oracle
- PADI International (SCUBA diving certification courses)
- The United States Office of Personnel Management
- Disney

There is no need to feel like you are taking a shortcut by using ACE-evaluated training for college credit. Remember, these training courses have been found to be comparable to college courses in both content and rigor. In addition, there are many well-known and highly-respected schools that accept ACE evaluated training. The following list represents just a small sample of the hundreds of schools that accept ACE evaluated training for college credit:

- The University of Alabama (Roll Tide!)
- The University of California—Berkeley
- Colorado State University
- The George Washington University
- Florida State University
- The University of Maine
- Johns Hopkins University
- The University of Massachusetts—Amherst
- Mississippi State University
- The University of Montana
- The University of New Mexico
- The University of North Dakota
- Ohio University
- The University of Oklahoma
- Pennsylvania State University
- George Mason University
- James Madison University

Turning Training Programs into College Credit

So, just how does one go about turning an ACE evaluated training program into college credit? The first step is simple…you first want to make sure your school accepts ACE evaluated credit. You can usually find this information right on your school's web site or in its academic policies. You can also check right on the ACE website itself since it has put together a convenient list of schools that accept ACE credit.

Just because your school accepts ACE credit doesn't mean it will accept every single ACE evaluated training program there is. Each school has its own policy on how many ACE evaluated college credits a student can use in a degree program and which training programs it will accept for credit. Some will allow you to use only a little ACE evaluated training toward a college degree, while others are more liberal in the number of ACE evaluated credits they will accept. Depending on the school and your particular major, you may be able to apply ACE evaluated credit to your general education requirements, electives, or even apply them to your major or minor. In some cases, ACE evaluated training programs may not seem like they fit anywhere. This is especially true for training programs that are highly technical or uncommon, like some military training programs. If this turns out to be the case, you might still be able to use them as electives credit. Be sure you've done your homework on becoming familiar with your school's ACE policy before proceeding.

How do you inform your school that you have ACE evaluated training? It's simple...you have it transcribed on an official ACE transcript and have it sent to your school. To obtain an ACE transcript, you first need to register with ACE (www.acenet.edu/transcripts). Registration is very easy and takes less than a minute to complete. From there you can select the organizations you have completed training through and the specific training programs you've completed and add them to your account. Once you select "submit for review," a request for training verification is then automatically sent to the organizations you listed. The review process takes between one to three days to complete and you'll receive an e-mail notification informing you of the outcome.

After you have all of your training listed on an ACE transcript, you can then order a copy and have it sent directly to your school. ACE charges $40 for the first transcript you order and $15 for each additional transcript.

When your school receives the ACE transcript, it will be treated the same as transfer credit from another school. As long as you have training on your ACE transcript that is in agreement with your school's ACE policy, and as long as it will fit in your degree plan, you should receive college credit for those courses.

A Closer Look at One Company and Its Training Program

So far we know it's possible to earn college credit for many different training programs that are held outside of the traditional college and university setting. We've also established that it's very easy to use portfolio assessment or to have that training documented on an official ACE transcript to be sent to your school as transfer credit. But what kind of college credit can you expect to earn from these training programs? The answer is…a little bit of everything. The list of possibilities is nearly as long as what most college course catalogs offer.

It is possible, however, to get an idea of what you can expect by taking a closer look at one company and the training programs it offers. Of all the organizations that participate in the ACE College Credit Recommendation Service, there is one that really stands out due to the sheer number of people who have worked for it. That company is McDonald's.

Hamburger University

So many people throughout the world have worked at McDonald's, at least at some point in their lives, that it's almost a rite of passage. The fast-food chain is a very popular place for many teenagers and young adults to earn supplemental income while pursuing their education. Many who start off working at McDonald's at a young age continue with the company and work their way up the chain as assistant manager, restaurant manager, and some even move on up to corporate.

There's no denying it…McDonald's knows a thing or two about business. As an early franchise pioneer, the restaurant chain was instrumental in the industry's adoption of process standardization and automation and literally created the model by which all fast-food restaurants follow today. As an industry leader, McDonald's takes the education of its employees very seriously. So seriously, in fact, that it has created one of the largest corporate training programs in the world. To ensure a well-trained workforce, McDonald's created Hamburger University, an institution with a funny-sounding name and a very serious mission (www.mcdonalds.com/usa/work/burgeru.html).

Hamburger University is located just outside of Chicago, Illinois, in a 130,000 square foot, state-of-the-art facility on an 80-acre campus. The modern school is a center of higher education in every way with interactive classrooms, laboratories, an auditorium, and even full-time instructors teaching in multiple languages. Thankfully, international students no longer have to travel to the United States for management training. The company has since opened Hamburger University branches in several countries. Training for junior managers is typically completed in regional training facilities, while advanced training is held at one of the Hamburger University training centers.

The training program at Hamburger University has nothing to do with burgers, fries, or a red-headed clown in a jumpsuit. Rather, the curriculum covers such common business topics as management, leadership, operations, finance, and others. The training at Hamburger University is of such a high quality that ACE has recommended a combined total of 46 credit hours of college credit for the courses offered. The thousands of people who graduate from a Hamburger University training program each year can use these credits toward the completion of an associate's or bachelor's degree from one of the many schools that accept ACE evaluated training. These credits could be applied toward a business major, a business minor, or even used as electives credit.

The following is a list of Hamburger University courses, the amount, and the type (upper or lower-division) of college credit for each course as recommended by ACE. It's also important to point out that when these courses are recorded on a college transcript, credit is usually awarded for their corresponding academic courses. The Operations Supervisor course, for example, would be recorded on a college transcript as three upper-level credits in either management, human resources management, or hospitality management. The training consultants course would be recorded as three lower-division credits in principles of management, training and development, or education. And so forth.

Course Title	**ACE Recommended College Credits**
Operations Supervisor	3/U
Operations Consultants Course	3/U
Financial Skills Development	2/U
Business Consultants MDP	3/U
Partnering for Results	2/U
Training Consultants Course	3/L
Delivery Skills for Presentation	1/L
Training Consultants Development Program	3/U

Managing the Organization	3/L
Foundations of Leadership	3/U
Developing a Global Mindset	1/L
Management Development Program 1	1/L
ServSafe	1/L
Basic Shift Management	1/L
Advanced Shift Management	1/L
Management Development Program 2	2/L
Effective Management Practices	3/L
Management Development Program 3	2/L
Restaurant Operations Leadership Practices	3/L
Management Development Program 4	2/U
Business Leadership Practices	3/L
Total	46

McDonald's has gone to great lengths to make sure its employees are aware of the potential to turn their Hamburger University training into college credit. To assist its employees in achieving their academic goals, the company has created a website called the McDonald's College Credit Connection, which provides general information on the process:
(www.aboutmcdonalds.com/mcd/careers/hamburger_university/collegecredit.html)

No Previous ACE Evaluated Training? No Problem.

If you are someone who doesn't have any corporate or volunteer training under your belt, you might be wondering how the concept of ACE evaluated credit could possibly apply to you. Although the temptation at this point may be to mentally categorize ACE credit in the "does not apply" section of your cranial filing cabinet, bear with me a little longer. Things are about to get very interesting.

In the next chapter we're going to look at a couple of organizations that offer some (very) inexpensive online courses that have been ACE evaluated for college credit. These are great opportunities you can pursue today, even if you have no current affiliation with the organizations offering the training.

CHAPTER 9

Big Savings on the Road Less Traveled

"If a man empties his purse into his head, no man can take it away from him. An investment in knowledge always pays the best interest."

– Ben Franklin

Portfolio assessment and ACE evaluated credit both represent incredible ways to turn prior learning experiences into usable college credit. Why not save big money and earn credit for what you already know at the same time? After all, having to take a formal college course just to earn credit in something you're already well-versed in is a real bummer. And a time waster. And it has the uncanny ability of making your bank account smaller, too. ACE and portfolio assessment give you the ability to earn the credit you deserve and put an end to inefficient repetition.

ACE doesn't always have to be about earning credit for prior learning experiences. Did you know there are many inexpensive online courses you can take right now that have been ACE evaluated for college credit? There are even a few online courses available that haven't been ACE evaluated but are accepted by some colleges for college credit. These are courses that are much more affordable than what most community colleges charge. And not only that, but some of them are free. Yes, free. As in…no charge.

Before you pursue any of the following strategies, definitely check with your school first to make sure it will accept them for college credit. By now it should be almost second nature to do so. After all, things change. Schools change their policies all the time. You can definitely save big money by using the following strategies but make sure your school gives you the "thumbs up" before attempting to incorporate them into your degree plan.

A Straighter Line to a College Degree

Straighterline (www.straighterline.com) is not the latest dance craze or some kind of abstract geometry problem. Rather, it is the name of a company with an entirely new model of higher education that has the potential to completely transform the college scene as we know it. The company offers more than 40 online courses in the traditional subjects that typically make up the first two years of a college degree (lower-division courses).

Straighterline, a for-profit company, takes an entirely different approach to higher education than the traditional model we're all used to. First of all, you are completely free to work at your own pace. Are you a fast learner? Straighterline's online courses can be completed as fast as you are able to work through them. And you don't have to wait for a new semester to begin to get started. There are no specific start or stop dates for any courses.

One of the most interesting things about Straighterline courses is how incredibly affordable they are. Students pay a flat fee of $99 per month plus a one-time enrollment fee per course of only $49. It doesn't matter how many courses you are taking at a time; the monthly fee is still only $99. This is more affordable than most community colleges! The $99 monthly fee can be discontinued at any time. A highly motivated student could sign up for two Straighterline courses and complete them in only one month for under $200. These same two courses at a private university could easily cost more than $2,000. Which one sounds like the better deal?

As great a deal as this is, it gets even better. Straighterline now offers a deal that lets you complete 10 courses (up to 30 credit hours) for a flat fee of only $1,299. This comes to approximately $43 per credit hour and is the equivalent of completing one-fourth of a bachelor's degree for less than what many people spend on one single college course.

How is Straighterline able to offer these courses for so little and be profitable? It's really just a matter of cutting out the unnecessary overhead that traditional schools have to deal with. There is no physical campus, sports stadiums, landscaping, exercise facilities, or any of those other expensive things. Straighterline has very little overhead. All courses are offered entirely online and are mostly automated, although there is plenty of help available from a real person should you need it. All Straighterline courses (with the exception of the English composition courses) require the completion of a proctored final exam.

There are two ways you can turn Straighterline courses into college credit. First, it's important to point out that Straighterline does not hold regional accreditation. However, all of the company's courses have been ACE evaluated for college credit. After completing all of the Straighterline courses you need, you can then have them recorded on an ACE transcript and sent to your school to be applied to your transcript (as long as your school accepts ACE evaluated credit).

In the second method you simply apply to one of Straighterline's partner schools for direct credit transfer. Straighterline has made arrangements with several colleges and universities that offer both traditional and online degree programs that allow you to complete many of the company's courses and have them applied directly to your transcript. The list of schools with Straighterline transfer agreements is continually growing.

Although the Straighterline model of education is still in its infancy, it is already a big success. And why wouldn't it be? Since the courses are entirely online and can be completed at your own pace, they are both convenient and affordable. You don't even have to wait for your class to keep up with you if you're a fast learner. Need to take a little more time on a particular subject? No problem. And of course, perhaps the most attractive feature of these courses is just how little they cost.

FEMA to the Rescue

Whenever you hear that something is being offered for free, do you automatically become suspicious? Does your internal "scam alert" start going off? If so, it's totally understandable. There's always a catch, right? That free sample leads to a high-pressure sales pitch to buy more of the same. That free seven-day trial that you forgot to cancel leads to a surprise charge on your credit card statement. What's a person to do? Is there anything in this world anymore that is truly free? Thankfully, yes.

What would you think if someone told you there is a U.S. federal agency that offers a series of free online courses that several colleges accept for college credit? Your first impression might be that it sounds too good to be true. It's no fantasy. It's the real deal. In fact, many people use these free courses each year as elective credits in their degree programs. Let's see how you can get in on it.

The Federal Emergency Management Agency (FEMA) is the federal agency in charge of responding to large-scale emergency situations and coordinating relief efforts. To provide a source of continuing education to emergency response officials and others who might be interested in the field, FEMA created the Emergency Management Institute (EMI) (http://training.fema.gov), a training center that offers over 400 courses in a variety of emergency-related topics. Most EMI courses are taught in-person at the institute's training center at Emmitsburg, Maryland, but quite a few online courses are offered as well. It's the online courses that we're interested in. The primary qualification for taking any of the free online FEMA courses is that you must be a United States citizen.

Although many of the FEMA courses that are offered in person have been ACE evaluated for college credit, none of the free online courses have this designation. Nevertheless, there are several schools that do accept them for college credit, including Thomas Edison State College, Charter Oak State College, Frederick Community College, and Bellevue University. Excelsior College also accepts the free online FEMA courses for college credit if they appear on an official transcript from another regionally accredited school. In other words, for lack of a better term, the credits must be laundered before Excelsior will accept them (more on this later).

Why bother even mentioning the free online FEMA courses if so few schools accept them for credit? They are worth mentioning because all three of the assessment schools accept them (we'll cover these three schools in the next chapter). These three colleges alone serve many thousands of nontraditional students, students who could definitely benefit from free FEMA credit. Bellevue University is another school that serves many nontraditional students. Although the university has a traditional campus in Bellevue, Nebraska, it is also a military-friendly school that offers many of its degree programs online.

How can the free online FEMA credits be used in a typical degree program? Very sparingly. It's unlikely that you will be able to use these credits in your major, minor, or for your general education requirements. You can, however, use them as electives credit. This is usually the only place they can be applied since most FEMA courses are in nonstandard subjects that usually don't appear in most college catalogs. We're talking about courses with names like Radiological Emergency Management, State Disaster Management, Livestock in Disasters, Building Partnerships with Tribal Governments, and others.

Taking Online FEMA Courses

Taking any of the online FEMA courses is very easy. There is no need to even submit an application. You simply find the course you want to take from the list and select it. You'll then see additional links that say "Download Materials," "Download Final Exam Questions," and "Take the Final Exam."

You'll first want to download and read all of the PDF files under the "Download Materials" link. This is the course content. Familiarize yourself well with these materials. After you have finished reading the course materials, you can then select "Download Final Exam Questions." This is the actual final exam. Answer each multiple-choice question and record your answers on paper.

Finally, select "Take the Final Exam." This leads you to a page that lets you submit your answers by selecting the appropriate radio button for each question. Since the actual questions are not found on this page, you will have to refer to the responses you previously recorded on paper. After selecting answers to all of the questions, there is a brief section where you fill out information about yourself. You then simply select "submit." That's it. You're done. FEMA will then send a certificate of completion to you via e-mail that you can print and keep for your records.

There are two ways to have your completed FEMA courses listed as college credit on your official transcript. The first is through direct credit transfer. If you are a student with either Thomas Edison State College, Charter Oak State College, or Bellevue University, consult with your student adviser for specifics on having your free FEMA credits added to your transcript. The second method involves paying a fee to have your free FEMA courses added to an official Frederick Community College transcript. This is the method you should use if you are either a Frederick Community College student or you want to have those credits added to your Excelsior College transcript.

Credit Laundering

For a fee of $76 per credit hour, Frederick Community College (www.frederick.edu) will record your online FEMA courses on an official transcript. You can then order a Frederick Community College transcript and have it sent to Excelsior College to have the credits applied to your Excelsior College transcript.

Having your online FEMA courses transcribed by Frederick Community College is very easy. From the school's emergency management degree program website (www.emergencymanagementstudy.com/content/default.asp) simply select the link marked "College Credit for IS Courses." From there you simply print the application form and submit it with your payment. As an added bonus, Frederick has a place right on the application that lets you designate the school you would like to have an official transcript sent to (credit laundering made easy). After the FEMA courses have been transcribed on your new Frederick transcript (which may take up to four weeks), Frederick will automatically send an official transcript to the school you designated.

Who says you can't get anything for free anymore? If you are a student at a school that accepts these credits as direct transfer and you have a few electives credits you need to fill, why not let FEMA come to the rescue and save you from spending any more on tuition than is absolutely necessary?

College Credit Through ALEKS

Algebra. Statistics. Math. The mere mention of these words is enough to cause many people to break out in a cold sweat. It's not hard to see why. In these challenging subjects, new lessons often build on the mastery of earlier concepts. A failure to learn just one or two of the many concepts a typical math course covers could cause a student to quickly fall behind. While some people are naturally gifted at math, others view these subjects as major obstacles that stand in the way of completing a college degree.

It's not uncommon for many people who are taking challenging math courses to need additional homework assistance after class. However, help is not always available when it's needed. If you realize you don't fully understand something while working on your homework assignment after class, where do you go for help? Your instructor probably doesn't want to be bothered after regular class or office hours. And if your friends or family aren't taking the course with you, they may not understand the subject enough to be of any real help, try as they may. If you wait until the class meets again to get assistance, it may be too late. The instructor may be ready to move on to a new topic, leaving you with an incomplete assignment and an incomplete understanding of the material.

Wouldn't it be great then if there was some kind of online tutor with an artificial intelligence that could adapt to your learning? A tutor you had access to anytime you want, even at 2:00 a.m.? This tutor would remember the things you've already mastered and wouldn't bother you with those things again. Instead, it would focus only on those things you need further help with, continually reassessing your mastery of the subject as you go along.

Such an online tutor does exist and its name is ALEKS (www.aleks.com), which stands for **A**ssessment and **LE**arning in **K**nowledge **S**paces. ALEKS was created as a joint venture between New York University and the University of California-Irvine, and was funded by the United States government (you, the taxpayer). As a taxpayer you spent a lot of money to develop ALEKS, so you may as well get some use out of it.

ALEKS is a very easy tool to use and all available courses are offered in either English or Spanish. The first time you log into an ALEKS course, you will be prompted to complete an assessment that is used to assess your current knowledge of the material. You can then begin working on the concepts you haven't yet mastered. The course learning modules are not multiple choice like other online study aids. Rather, you must input data and solve problems in a manner similar to working out problems the traditional way.

One of the truly great things about the ALEKS system is that several of the online courses have been ACE evaluated for college credit. This means you can work through an ALEKS course from the comfort of your home and receive college credit for it from a school that accepts ACE evaluated credit. ALEKS courses are listed on the ACE website under "ALEKS Corporation (McGraw Hill)." The following is a list of ALEKS courses that have been ACE evaluated for college credit:

- Beginning Algebra
- Intermediate Algebra
- College Algebra
- College Algebra with Trigonometry
- Pre-Calculus
- Trigonometry
- Introduction to Statistics
- Business Statistics
- Statistics for the Behavioral Sciences

ALEKS is designed to take a student all the way from no knowledge of the material to complete mastery of the subject. Thankfully though, it isn't necessary to completely master a subject to earn college credit. All you need to do is complete an assessment to a level of at least 70 percent. A grade of 70 percent is typically a "C" at most schools. And since most schools that accept ACE credit will assign a "Pass" or "CR" on your transcript instead of a letter grade, a 70 is just as good as a 100. If by some chance you pass your first assessment at 70 percent or greater…that's it. You're done! You can then have the course added to your ACE transcript. Although you can continue working on an ALEKS course until you reach 100 percent on an assessment, it isn't necessary.

Working your way through an ALEKS online course is neither quick nor easy. ALEKS makes absolutely sure you've learned the material before moving on. You can plan on putting in anywhere from 40 to 60 hours on each course, depending on your knowledge of the subject before starting. Still, a highly-motivated student could complete one of these courses in under a month.

Most people who start working on an ALEKS course are not going to reach an assessment of 70 percent the first time. It's okay if you don't. ALEKS was designed to get you up to speed on the course material one module at a time. One week into the course you may only be at 36 percent, while a week later you may be at 49 percent. Just keep plugging away at it and soon enough you'll reach an assessment level of 70 percent.

One of the most interesting aspects of ALEKS courses is just how little they cost. ALEKS charges a monthly fee of only $20 per course and you get the first two days free to try it out. Yes, you read that right, only $20! If it takes you a little more than a month to complete a course, you will simply be charged another $20. It is essentially a monthly subscription that you can cancel at any time. Let's see…$20 for an ACE evaluated ALEKS math course or $600-$1,500 for the same course from your local college. Not a tough choice, is it?

Inexpensive ALEKS courses are something that many can benefit from. They are easy to access, convenient, and cheaper than an evening out at the movies. If you haven't already completed the algebra and statistics courses you need for your degree, definitely check with your school to see if these will work. If your school accepts ACE evaluated courses for college credit (which many schools do), you can use this strategy to save big money.

Today's superhighways are packed with weary travelers making their way to their destinations, their only goal being to get from point A to point B. How much more interesting would those car trips be if they were on a back country road? How much more scenic? How many people even bother to consider an alternate route? In many ways higher education is the same way. The most commonly traveled road that students take while pursuing their college degrees involves taking traditional college courses from start to finish and funding them with student loans. How many of these students even realize there are alternate roads that lead to the same academic destination? How many realize there are strategies that let you earn the exact same college degree without going deep in debt? Too few.

The road less traveled is always worth checking out, regardless of your goals and pursuits. For those pursuing a college degree, it means earning college credits more quickly and for much less money than they would by taking traditional college courses. Why spend any more than you have to for the exact same college credits? Consider the road less traveled for big savings.

CHAPTER 10

The Assessment Schools

"If opportunity doesn't knock, build a door."

– Milton Berle

Barriers To A College Degree

Earning a college degree the traditional way is easier said than done for many people. This is especially true for those who have to work full time to pay the mortgage, buy groceries, take care of the kids, and do all of those other things that responsible adults are supposed to take care of. The very thought of quitting work and going to school full time for many working adults is almost laughable.

There are also many people who don't have the luxury of staying in one place long enough to earn a college degree. They may take a few courses at one school before their job (or the military) transfers them to a new location, where they complete a few more courses at a new school before they are transferred yet again. Since most schools require the completion of at least 30 credit hours taken in their system to graduate with a bachelor's degree, students who move often may not be able to fulfill this requirement, leaving them with many college credits but no practical way of finishing their degrees.

There are also many people who decide to earn a college degree after spending years in the workforce. Although they may be highly competent in their careers, they may not be able to effectively compete with others for a promotion without a college degree. Yes, there was a time when you could move up the corporate ladder with hard work, dedication, seniority, and experience, but the times are definitely changing.

Although there are many career options that don't require a college degree at all (we discussed this in the first chapter), it's also true that many companies now require you to have that piece of paper that says you are an associate of something or a bachelor of something else before you can be promoted. This is a fairly new development in the workforce and is the result of more and more people graduating from college. Some refer to it as "credential creep." It is a term that describes a situation where more credentials are now required to do the same kind of work that could be done with fewer credentials (or none) in years past.

Those who decide to earn a college degree mid-career, as well as students in situations that prevent them from attending school on a full-time basis, are often referred to as nontraditional students. They have different needs, experiences, and learning styles than students who attend college straight out of high school. They also have job, family, and community commitments and often find attending traditional college courses difficult, if not impossible.

A Flexible College for Nontraditional Students

What many nontraditional students really need is a different kind of college…a college that was designed specifically to meet the needs and challenges of adult students. Such a college would let them transfer in all of their previously earned college credits (as long as they are from schools with regional accreditation). The school would also accept many different sources of nontraditional credits such as challenge exams (CLEP, DSST, etc.), portfolio assessment, and ACE evaluated training. No restrictions would be placed on previously earned credits due to how long ago they were earned or what subjects they were in, giving students the ability to get maximum mileage out of all previously completed courses. Such a college would let its students transfer in all degree requirements for a particular major from other schools, with the exception of one or two courses (which could be conveniently taken online), and then graduate.

The Assessment Schools

The good news for nontraditional students is that there are actually three of these highly-flexible schools to choose from. These schools are commonly referred to as the "assessment schools" since they primarily assess college credits earned through other schools and through nontraditional sources and then award a college degree when all degree requirements are met. The three assessment schools include Excelsior College (New York), Charter Oak State College (Connecticut), and Thomas Edison State College (New Jersey).

Today, these colleges are thriving institutions of higher learning that continually receive recognition for their innovative programs that increase access to higher education. Many thousands of people from around the world have earned degrees from these schools and have gone on to pursue graduate degrees in every field imaginable, even from some of the most prestigious schools. These three assessment schools have opened the previously locked doors of higher education to many who otherwise couldn't have attended a traditional school to pursue their dream of earning a college degree.

An Affordable Option

In addition to offering access to higher education for the nontraditional student, the assessment schools are easily among the most affordable schools in all of higher education. They are truly a remarkable deal. It's possible to earn an associate's degree from Charter Oak State College, for example, for not much more than the price of a typical week-long vacation for two. Check out the following breakdown of expenses using CLEP exams and Straighterline courses (which Charter Oak accepts as direct transfer) to see just how affordable this can be:

Charter Oak State College Application Fee	$75
College Semester Fee (one semester only)	228
Charter Oak State College Cornerstone Course	966
30 credit hours through Straighterline	1,299
5 CLEP Exams Worth 6 Credit Hours Each ($77×5)	385
CLEP Transcript	20
Graduation Fee	205
Grand Total for Associate's Degree	$3,178

The fees and tuition shown in the example are for out-of-state residents. If you're a resident of Connecticut or on active duty in the military, you'll pay even less. Also, this scenario assumes you're starting the program without any previously earned credits. If you already have some college credit, have completed ACE evaluated training, or believe you can earn some credits through portfolio assessment, your total expenses can be even less.

Increased Opportunities for Portfolio Assessment

Do you recall where we discussed in a previous chapter about how you can only use portfolio assessment to earn college credit in courses offered by your school? Things are a bit different with the assessment schools. All three of the assessment schools offer portfolio assessment; however, instead of limiting you to only earning college credit in courses that each of the three schools offer, they let you submit portfolios for courses offered by other schools.

There are two ways you can use this to your advantage. First, you can use this strategy to earn college credit in obscure subjects that you happen to have college-level knowledge in. Excelsior College may not offer courses in such uncommon subjects as bluegrass music, old-time music, storytelling, or Appalachian studies, but guess what...East Tennessee State University does. If you have specialized knowledge in these subjects and have the evidence to prove it, you can submit portfolios in these subjects to Excelsior College based on the courses offered by East Tennessee State University and earn college credit in these subjects.

Second, not all schools award the same amount of college credit for each course. There are some schools that may award three credit hours for fundamentals of equine studies (the study of horses) while another school may offer four credit hours for the same course. If you are interested in earning portfolio assessment credit in a particular course and you discover some schools award more credit than others, why not submit a portfolio based on the school that awards the higher number of credits? Guess which one I'd choose?

Military Friendly

Are you on active duty or in the reserves of any branch of the U.S. military? If so, your out-of-pocket expense for a degree through one of the assessment schools can be reduced to zero. Yes, zero…as in zilch. Nada. Nothing. A free degree. There are a few factors in play that make this possible.

First, all CLEP and DSST challenge exams are completely free for active-duty military personnel as well as those in the reserves and National Guard. They are paid for by the Department of Defense. Second, the assessment schools are very generous in accepting military training programs that have been ACE evaluated. If you've completed basic training and additional training for your military occupational specialty (MOS), you might be surprised at how many ACE evaluated credits you've already earned. Lastly, military personnel have both military tuition assistance and the GI Bill to pay for any additional courses or college fees.

The assessment schools are often considered to be some of the most military-friendly schools there are. In fact, some of the degree programs offered by the assessment schools were designed specifically for military personnel. These degree programs were designed to make maximum usage of the ACE evaluated military training programs already completed.

Just to give you an idea of what you can expect from your military training, Thomas Edison State College awards 60 credit hours for the completion of the FAA Air Traffic Control Specialist certification. This is half of a bachelor's degree! Other examples include the FAA Airframe and Powerplant Certification (67 credits), FAA Repairman Certificate (65 credits), Navy Basic Nuclear Power School (41 credits), Navy Qualifications Beyond Basic Nuclear Power School (3-20 credits), and many others.

If you are enrolling in a degree program offered by one of the assessment schools and you are in the military, be sure to let them know of your military status up front. Your academic adviser can assist you in making the best use of the military training you've completed in your degree plan. Many service members are often surprised to learn just how close to finishing a degree they are when their military training is factored in. In the military, a college degree means higher pay and rank advancement. Don't miss out!

Accredited and Respected

It's important to keep in mind that the three assessment schools hold regional accreditation, the gold standard of collegiate accreditation in the United States. Charter Oak State College, for example, is accredited by the New England Association of Schools and Colleges, the same agency that accredits Yale, Harvard, Dartmouth, and Brown. Thomas Edison State College and Excelsior College are accredited by the Middle States Association of Colleges and Schools, the same agency that accredits Princeton, Columbia, Cornell, and Johns Hopkins. A degree from any of the three assessment schools can open many doors in your life, both in your career and future graduate studies.

Let's go ahead now and take a closer look at each of the three assessment schools. Although they are very similar in how they operate, there are enough differences to make each one unique. Since we've already seen an example of a degree plan through Charter Oak State College, we'll lead off with that school...

Charter Oak State College

Founded in 1973 in the city of New Britain, Connecticut, Charter Oak State College (www.charteroak.edu) is one of Connecticut's state colleges and was named after the state's historical "Charter Oak." Charter Oak State College does not have a traditional campus, per se, where students gather and take courses. Rather, the school's students are found all over the world. Students can earn their degrees through Charter Oak from a distance without ever visiting New Britain. The school's physical presence consists of office buildings for administrators, advisers, and the storage of student records.

Charter Oak State College allows students to transfer in almost all of the credits needed to complete an associate's degree, with the exception of a cornerstone course that must be completed through their system to graduate. For a bachelor's degree, students can transfer in all of the credits needed to graduate with the exception of the cornerstone course and a capstone course, both of which can be completed entirely online. Charter Oak permits students to use many different sources of college credit to complete their degrees, including challenge exams (CLEP, DSST, etc.), ACE evaluated training, portfolio assessment, military training, and of course, any previously earned college credits from regionally accredited schools. Charter Oak also offers over 150 online courses of its own. To enroll in a Charter Oak State College degree program, you must be at least 16 years old and have already completed nine credit hours (which can be fulfilled with challenge exams).

Concentrations Only

All of the degrees offered by Charter Oak State College, both at the associate's and bachelor's degree level, are in general studies with a concentration in a specific field of study. What is the difference between a concentration and a major? At most schools a major will have a very rigid list of courses you must take to fulfill the degree requirements. Most majors require between 30 to 36 credit hours to complete. Of these, typically only six to nine credit hours may be in electives specific to the major.

A concentration, on the other hand, allows much more freedom in choosing courses that interest you. A concentration in biology, for example, may only require 15 credit hours in core biology courses while the remaining 15 to 21 credit hours could be in biology electives that are more suited to your interests. In the end you'll have a degree in the subject of your choice, whether it's with a major or concentration. Rarely does it matter which one you go with. Concentrations are available in nearly 50 areas of study.

Design Your Own Degree

One of Charter Oak's most popular concentrations is the individualized studies degree program. This is the closest thing to a "design your own degree" there is. It allows for great flexibility in degree completion and enables students to draw from more than one discipline to fulfill their concentration requirements. If you're interested in e-commerce, for example, you could create an individualized studies concentration and take courses in business, computer science, and marketing. There are many possibilities. You can really get creative with this one.

Charter Oak State College offers a truly flexible way to earn a college degree at a very affordable price. The school holds regional accreditation, is one of Connecticut's state colleges, and is accessible from anywhere in the world, at anytime.

Now, let's see what those guys in New York are up to…

Excelsior College

Established in 1971, in Albany, New York, Excelsior College (www.excelsior.edu) is a private, nonprofit college offering associate's, bachelor's, and masters degrees in many different subjects. The college was established by the University of the State of New York (USNY), the state agency that is responsible for overseeing all of New York's colleges and universities and ensuring they meet state standards. It's the state's Board of Regents. USNY was originally created in 1784 to oversee a quaint, little school you may have heard of, Columbia University.

From State College to Private, Nonprofit College

Although Excelsior College is now a private, nonprofit college, it started off as a state college. For many years the school's degrees and diplomas were awarded under the University of the State of New York name. The college was first known as the Regents External Degree Program, a rather awkward name that probably didn't have too many fans. In 1984 the school adopted the name, Regents College, to reflect its status as a creation of the state's Board of Regents (a much better choice).

In 1998 it was decided that the school had matured to the point that it could spread its wings and fly on its own. That year the college was given an independent charter and separated from USNY. That new charter included the requirement to come up with a new name, and Excelsior College was the winning nomination. In case you're wondering, "Excelsior" is New York's state motto which means "ever upward." If you look up a picture of New York's state flag, you'll see the word "Excelsior" written across it in large, bold letters. It works.

Like Charter Oak, Excelsior College's students are found all over the globe. Where you live on the third rock from the sun is never a limitation if you are an assessment school student. There's never any need to visit the school's offices in Albany for any reason, even for graduation. Excelsior College allows you to transfer in nearly 100 percent of the credits needed to graduate and offers degree and certificate programs in nearly 50 areas of study.

Transfer In Almost All of Your Credits to Graduate

Excelsior College used to permit all of the credits needed for a degree to be transferred in from other sources but this has changed somewhat in recent years. Fortunately, very few of the credits required to graduate need to be taken through the college. The biggest downside to this change is that it will cost a little more to graduate than it would if you could have transferred in all of your credits from other sources. Nevertheless, when compared to most other schools, it's still a bargain.

How many courses will you need to take through Excelsior to graduate? Only two. You can transfer in all of the credits needed for both an associate's degree and a bachelor's degree with the exception of a one-credit course in information literacy and a three-credit capstone course.

Both of these courses can be completed online through Excelsior.

Like Charter Oak, there are many different sources of college credit you can use to complete an Excelsior College degree. Available options include transferring in credits from other schools with regional accreditation, ACE evaluated training, challenge exams (CLEP, DSST, etc.), and portfolio assessment. You can also take many courses online directly through Excelsior. The college charges $390 per credit hour for its online courses; however, if you are in the military, reserve, National Guard, or are a military spouse, you get a reduced rate of $250 per credit hour.

Excelsior College offers both concentrations and majors, depending on the degree program you are interested in. The major is the more traditional route, while the concentration gives you greater flexibility to take more courses that interest you. Graduate schools typically don't care which one you have as long as you have completed the necessary prerequisites for their programs. Some degree programs, like Excelsior's nursing program, only offer a major. This is because there are many specific courses that must be completed to sit for the state nursing exam. A concentration in this case just wouldn't work.

The Largest Nursing Program in the Nation

One very noteworthy aspect of Excelsior College is that it has the largest nursing program in the United States. There are Excelsior College registered nurses working in hospitals throughout the country and around the world. Chances are strong that your local hospital has several Excelsior College registered nurses working there now.

Excelsior's nursing program is highly regarded and has earned program accreditation by the National League for

Nursing Accrediting Commission (NLNAC). In fact, it's the only program of its kind that allows you to complete the academic part of a nursing degree and qualify to take National Counsel Licensure Examination (NCLEX) to become a registered nurse (mostly) by distance study.

Become a registered nurse by distance study? Is this safe? What about the clinical requirements that traditional RN programs require? Don't worry. Excelsior College has this all figured out. In order to qualify for admission into Excelsior's RN program, you must already be one of the following:

- Licensed Practical or Vocational Nurse (LPN or LVN)
- Paramedic
- Military Corpsman
- Respiratory Therapist
- Midwife
- Physician
- Licensed Psychiatric Technician (Arkansas and Colorado residents only)
- Transfer nursing students who have completed at least 50% of their clinical rotations with a "C" average within the last five years

So, you can see that those who qualify for entry into Excelsior's RN program already have substantial clinical experience. They won't be as green as the grass. And there are no worries about having to learn how to start IVs by distance study. If you are admitted into Excelsior's RN program, you will already have substantial medical experience and will know your way around a hospital quite well.

Excelsior College offers associate's, bachelor's, and master's degrees in nursing. The associate in science in nursing degree (ASN) is usually all you need to sit for the RN licensing exam but it's always good to check with your state's licensing board just to be sure. The bachelor of science in nursing (BSN) program is intended to further a registered nurse's education and does not require any additional clinical rotations or skills assessments. The BSN requires 121 credit hours to graduate, 60 of which are in nursing and the remainder in general education. Excelsior's ASN and BSN degree programs are both very flexible and allow for the use of a lot of inexpensive challenge exam credit.

Excelsior College also offers a Master of Science in Nursing (MSN) in clinical systems management, nursing education, or nursing informatics. Also offered is a graduate certificate in nursing management and a post-master's certificate in nursing education. And if you are so inclined, as an Excelsior nursing student you can even join the nursing honor society, Sigma Theta Tau International. As the nation's largest nursing school, Excelsior College has the whole nursing thing down.

An Exam to Verify You Know Your Stuff

In addition to already having substantial clinical experience, all Excelsior College nursing students must take and pass a rigorous clinical exam at the end of the program. This is a testament to the quality of the program since most RN programs don't even require a comprehensive exam such as this.

The Clinical Performance in Nursing Exam (CPNE) evaluates a student's ability to do all of the basic functions of a registered nurse. It is a skills assessment where students must demonstrate such things as starting IVs, giving shots, patient evaluations, and other critical nursing skills. The CPNE is an exam that must be taken in person. Thankfully though, you don't have to travel to Albany to take it. There are several CPNE test sites set up in various locations around the country.

Sources of Nursing Credit

Other than transferring in completed nursing credits from other schools, Excelsior's nursing students can earn college credits by completing nursing challenge exams or online courses. For the associate's degree in nursing, however, no online courses are offered, only exams. All nursing courses are upper-level and are intended to be used in the nursing bachelor's degree program.

As it turns out, though, the challenge exams are a much better deal. The exams range from $95 to $330 for anywhere from three to as many as eight credit hours per exam ($32 to $110 per credit hour). We've already covered Excelsior College's challenge exams in a previous chapter in case you need to go back for a quick review.

Let's Talk About the Cost

Enrollment in an Excelsior College degree program starts with an $80 preliminary review of your existing credits. After submitting the $80 fee and forwarding all existing transcripts to the school, you will receive an evaluation that shows where you currently stand and what you still lack to complete your degree.

There are two different tracks you can take with the enrollment fee. In the first option, you are required to complete at least 12 credit hours of course work through Excelsior to get a discounted enrollment fee of $395. This is the option to take if you plan on taking four or more courses through Excelsior College. The second option, at $1,015, does not require you to complete any Excelsior College courses and is definitely the way to go if you are transferring in the majority of your credits. The second option is ideal if you only need to take the one-credit course in information literacy and the capstone course.

For each year you are enrolled in Excelsior College you are required to pay an annual student advisory fee of $485. You can avoid paying this fee more than once by mapping out your degree plan prior to enrollment and then enrolling only when you're sure you can complete the degree in one year or less. This is not as hard as it may sound. That $80 preliminary review tells you exactly what additional courses you need to complete before you can graduate. With this information you can take affordable courses from other schools or challenge exams and then enroll when you're near the completion of all of your degree requirements. This also works for Excelsior's challenge exams since you don't have to be an enrolled student to take any of them, even the nursing exams.

Finally, Excelsior College's graduation fee is $495. There really is no way around this one. If you want that pretty piece of paper hanging on your wall in a fancy frame, you'll have to pony up for the graduation fee.

Excelsior's nursing students have one special fee they should plan for. The CPNE, the clinical performance in nursing examination, is priced at $2,145. This isn't cheap but the return on your investment with a degree in nursing and a state license as a registered nurse makes it totally worth it.

Here's a summary of Excelsior's fees for an associate's degree (non-nursing) so you can get the big picture. This assumes you are transferring in all of your credits except for the information literacy course and the capstone course:

Preliminary review	$80
Enrollment fee	1,015
Annual Student Advisory Fee	485
One-credit information literacy course	390
Capstone Course	1,170
Graduation fee	495
Total	$3,635

Affordable prices, flexible ways to earn credit, and the nation's largest nursing program make Excelsior College an undeniably great school. What's not to like?

Thomas Edison State College

Established in 1972 in Trenton, New Jersey, Thomas Edison State College (www.tesc.edu) is one of New Jersey's 12 state colleges. The college offers associate's and bachelor's degrees in more than 100 subjects, in addition to several master's degree programs. Like Charter Oak State College and Excelsior College, students don't have to visit the school for any reason. Thomas Edison State College students are found all across the nation and all around the world. Thomas Edison has been called a "best buy" in higher education on multiple occasions from some very respectable publications.

A Generous Credit Transfer Policy

Thomas Edison State College accepts a variety of recognized sources of college credit such as courses taken at regionally accredited schools, challenge exams, ACE evaluated training, portfolio assessment, and others. Interestingly, Thomas Edison also accepts more lower-division community college credit than is the norm. While most schools will accept around 60 credit hours of community college credit in transfer, Thomas Edison will accept up to 80 credit hours. This represents tremendous financial savings since community college credit is usually much more affordable than credit from a four-year college or university. All of Thomas Edison's undergraduate degree programs require the completion of a capstone course to graduate, which can be conveniently taken online.

Additional Sources of Low-Cost Credits

Thomas Edison State College is very receptive to challenge exam credit (CLEP, DSST, etc.) and has even developed its own challenge exams for a variety of courses. Known as the Thomas Edison State College Examination Program (TECEP), they are a great deal at only $99 per three-credit course for all students.

Thomas Edison also offers nearly 300 online or guided study courses in many different subjects that are very reasonably priced. If you know up front that you will need to take at least 36 credit hours to complete your degree, you can sign up for a package deal. Out-of-state students can pay an up-front fee of $7,837 for 36 credit hours worth of courses in the first year. If an additional 36 credit hours are needed, the price drops to $6,817 in the second year. This works out to the very reasonable prices of $218 and $189 per credit hour, respectively.

Thomas Edison courses are an even better deal if you are a New Jersey resident or are in the military (the same price applies to both). These students can get a package deal of 36 credit hours for $5,322 in the first year ($148 per credit hour) and $4,432 in the second year ($123 per credit hour). A true and rare bargain in the world of higher education.

Must Be 21 to Enroll

To enroll in any Thomas Edison degree program you must be at least 21 years old and hold a high school diploma or GED. Why 21 years old? Thomas Edison probably wants to emphasize that its degree programs are intended for adults instead of the straight-out-of-high-school crowd. Now, having said that, there's nothing stopping you from earning college credits from a variety of affordable sources and then enrolling with Thomas Edison to complete your degree on your 21st birthday.

Let's Not Forget the Fees

With the exception of the annual enrollment fee, Thomas Edison's fees are very affordable. You can avoid paying the annual enrollment fee more than once by completing the majority of your degree requirements prior to enrolling to ensure you can complete the remainder in one year or less. The following is a breakdown of Thomas Edison's fees for all degree-seeking students:

Application Fee	$75
Technology Services Fee	117
Annual Enrollment Fee	2,958
Graduation Fee	280
Total	$3,430

Three Great Choices

Charter Oak, Excelsior, and Thomas Edison all stand out as exceptional deals in a world of high-dollar higher education. If you choose to pursue a college degree through any of the three assessment schools, you can rest assured that the degree you earn will be widely accepted and respected, both by employers and by those in graduate school admissions. These two state colleges and one private, nonprofit college allow you to earn an undergraduate degree for much less than what most people spend on the exact same degree at other schools. You can then use the money you saved to pay for a master's degree, or make a down payment on a home, or take a much-needed vacation after earning your degree, or…

You get the idea.

CHAPTER 11

Join the Military for a Free College Degree

"Do not accustom yourself to consider debt only as an inconvenience; you will find it a calamity."

– Samuel Johnson

Awake at 0400 hours, dealing with an angry drill sergeant, and a five-mile hike before most people even start their days. Such is life in the military, right? Well, sort of. But not entirely. While it's true you will have to go through a program of basic training, regardless of which branch you join, today's high-tech military is much different than what it was even just a few decades ago. It's certainly not the military your grandfather would recall. And if you've been watching the classic flick, *Full Metal Jacket*, to get an idea of what life in the military is like, hit eject on your movie player, disregard any preconceived notions you may have, and let's take a good look at the opportunities available in today's modern military.

Opportunities Abound

An enlistment in the military equals opportunity. And not in just one or two areas, either. There are so many opportunities available in today's modern military, it makes many other options pale in comparison. This is especially true if you are someone who is just starting out in life after graduating from high school. Some of the many opportunities available include free career training, valuable work experience, out-of-this-world benefits, and many others.

Joining the military is a great way to jump start a career. While you can still train to be a professional soldier, there are many military career paths you can pursue that are also highly valuable in the civilian world. A few examples include computer information systems, aviation, medical, financial, communications, education, engineering, environmental, intelligence, law enforcement, logistics, and many others. As you can see, many military career paths are very similar to those you would find in civilian life.

Your military training and experience will be highly desired when you rejoin the civilian workforce after your military career. If you apply for a civilian job with the federal government and you have military experience, you automatically get a bonus added to your overall applicant score that can make a big difference in landing that highly-prized government job. And not only that but military experience is viewed very favorably by civilian employers as well. Employers know that military experience is high-quality experience. Which do you think looks better on a resume: six years serving in the Navy on a high-tech naval vessel or six years working checkout at the local big box store? Not too hard to figure that one out, is it?

One of the truly great things about today's military is that you receive all of the training for your military career during your enlistment. This is free training that you would have had to spend many thousands of dollars to obtain as a civilian. And you receive full pay while you're training for your new career, too.

If free career training in the military isn't reason enough to consider joining, the benefits you'll receive while serving should definitely get your attention. In fact, few civilian organizations even come close to matching the breadth of benefits offered to military personnel. If you enlist in any branch of the U.S. military, you'll get excellent healthcare coverage, low-cost life insurance, special travel arrangements that let you fly very inexpensively (or free), several weeks of paid vacation each year, and many others. As an extra fringe benefit, you could even be stationed in some truly exciting, exotic places and get to see the world on the government's tab.

There are many people who decide to stay in the military after their initial enlistment is up and make a career out of it. It's easy to see why. It's hard to beat the retirement package. In the U.S. military, after you've put in a minimum of 20 years, you can call it quits and begin receiving retirement pay from your military pension. Think about it…retirement before you even reach your 40th birthday! Although most people who "retire" after 20 years in the military usually start new careers in the civilian sector, the extra income from their military pensions can really make a big difference to their bottom lines.

The military benefits we just discussed are in a league of their own and are often reason enough for many people to join. But there's one category of benefits we haven't yet mentioned that is truly remarkable. We're talking, of course, about the educational benefits available to military personnel. These are benefits that are almost unheard of in the civilian sector. What if I told you it's possible to join the military with zero college credits and earn an associate's degree, bachelor's degree, or higher while the

U.S. government picks up the tab? Think that might be worth checking out? Let's take a look at the many educational opportunities available to military personnel...

Free Challenge Exams for Military Personnel

Challenge exams are one of the most affordable ways to earn college credit there is. By taking only one exam you can earn three, six, or more college credits in a single day. They are so inexpensive you could earn 30 credit hours of challenge exam credit for under $1,000. That's one-fourth of a bachelor's degree for less money than many people spend on one single mortgage payment. As incredible a deal as this is, it gets even better if you are in the military.

If you are on active duty in any branch of the U.S. military or are in the reserves or National Guard, CLEP and DSST exams are completely free. No charge. They are paid for by the U.S. Department of Defense. How's that for a great deal? It's hard to beat anything that's free, isn't it? Your only expense will be the small fee you'll have to pay to order a CLEP or DSST transcript when you're finished taking all of the challenge exams you need for your degree.

College Credit for Military Training

We've already briefly talked about turning military training into usable college credit in a previous chapter. This information is so valuable, however, that it's worth a closer look. Through the ACE College Credit Recommendation Service, you can receive college credit for many military training programs by enrolling in a degree program through a college or university that accepts ACE evaluated credit. Just by completing basic training and training for your military occupation, you may already be well on your way toward the completion of a college degree.

How many military training programs have been ACE evaluated for college credit? Literally hundreds. So many military courses have been evaluated, in fact, that ACE has devoted an entire section of its website just to military personnel (http://militaryguides.acenet.edu).

Let's take a quick look at just a few military training programs that have been ACE evaluated and the amount of college credit (in semester hours) ACE recommends to get an idea of what you can expect. This is just a small sample of the hundreds of military training programs available:

Military Training Program	**ACE Credit Recommendation**
Military Police Investigations (Army)	6/L
Turkish Language Training I (Army)	12/L
Accounting (Army)	17/L
Civil Affairs (Army)	9/U
Alcoholism Treatment Specialist (Navy)	12/U
Pharmacy Technician (Navy)	4/L
Basic Flight Engineer (Navy)	2/U
Communications Supervisor (Navy)	6/L
Auditor (Air Force)	8/U
Computer Operator (Air Force)	4/U
Operating Room Nursing (Air Force)	19/U

Weather Observer Technician (Air Force)	6/U
Hospital Corpsman (Coast Guard)	6/L
Search and Rescue (Coast Guard)	4/L
Celestial Navigation (Coast Guard)	3/L
Fire Prevention (Coast Guard)	3/L
Basic Military Training (Marine Corp)	8/L
Basic Radar (Marine Corp)	4/L
Basic Reconnaissance (Marine Corp)	8/L
Data Network Specialist (Marine Corp)	8/L

After completing basic training and training for your military occupation, you could easily have 20, 30, or more ACE evaluated credits that you can apply to your college transcript. If you enroll in a degree program with a "military friendly" school, you can make maximum use of these credits toward the completion of your degree.

Military Transcripts

If you plan on taking advantage of using your ACE evaluated military training for college credit (and why wouldn't you?), your school will need some way to verify that you did, in fact, complete some military training. This is not a problem. You order a copy of your military transcript and have it sent to your school. Just as simple as that. You can also have your military training recorded on an ACE transcript. Check with your school to see which one it prefers.

Many service men and women are unaware that all of the training they receive while in the military is automatically recorded on a transcript. And I do mean *everything*. Basic training, advanced training, refresher training…it's all automatically recorded. It's really no different than having the courses you take in college recorded on your college transcript. You don't need to do anything to make it happen. Everything is recorded automatically. And you can very easily order a copy of this transcript and have it sent to your school.

Each branch of the military has its own transcript service, with the exception of the Navy and the Marines, which use the same service. You will need to order your transcript from the appropriate service, depending on which military branch you serve(d) in. There is no charge for any military transcript.

U.S. Army

If you serve(d) in the U.S. Army as an enlisted personnel (not a commissioned officer), you will need to order your military transcript from the Army American Registry Transcript System (AARTS) (https://aartstranscript.army.mil).

If you serve(d) as an officer in the U.S. Army, you will need to submit form DD 295 (http://images.military.com/Resources/Forms/DD_295.pdf).

U.S. Navy and Marines

If you serve(d) in the U.S. Navy or the U.S. Marines, regardless of rank, you will need to order your military transcript from the Sailor/Marine American Counsel on Education Registry Transcript (SMART) (https://smart.navy.mil/smart/welcome.do).

To order your transcript, you will need to fill out and submit the Official SMART Request Form (https://smart.navy.mil/request.pdf).

U.S. Air Force

Transcripts are handled a little bit differently in the U.S. Air Force. If you serve(d) in the U.S. Air Force, regardless of rank, you will need to order your military transcript from the Community College of the Air Force (CCAF) (www.au.af.mil/au/ccaf).

U.S. Coast Guard

Finally, if you serve(d) in the U.S. Coast Guard, regardless of rank, you will need to order your military transcript from the Coast Guard Institute (www.uscg.mil/hq/cgi/ve/official_transcript.asp).

Military Friendly Schools

If you are on active duty in any branch of the U.S. military, you will definitely want to enroll in a degree program with a college or university that is "military friendly." This designation simply means the school awards a generous amount of college credit for ACE evaluated military training programs. Many of these schools also offer degree programs that can be completed entirely online. This is an important consideration for any service member. You don't want to have to worry about being transferred to a new location and having to leave your school behind. With an online degree program, as long as you have an Internet connection, you can continue your studies from anywhere in the world.

Finding a military friendly school isn't difficult at all. In fact, the military friendly schools have formed a consortium called the Servicemembers Opportunity Colleges (SOC) (www.soc.aascu.org/) to help you easily identify them. The SOC is made up of approximately 1,900 colleges and universities. With such a large pool of schools to choose from, you're certain to find one that fits your needs.

While many of the SOCs offer online degree programs, you may have to do a little research to find a school with just the right degree program you're interested in. The best way to narrow down your choices and to find the right degree program for your needs is to contact your base's education center and tell them what you're interested in. They can help you narrow your choices down to a few great options. The military education centers are great assets. Use them.

Military Tuition Assistance

After finding the ideal military friendly school, applying your military training to your degree plan, and taking as many challenge exams as your school will allow, you'll still have to take a certain number of college courses to fulfill your degree requirements. But how do you pay for these courses? You can pay for any additional courses you need by taking advantage of military tuition assistance.

Military tuition assistance is an incredible benefit that will pay for some or all of your tuition while you are on active duty in any branch of the U.S. military. These benefits are also available to reserve and National Guard personnel. In addition to paying for your tuition, this benefit can also be used to pay for lab fees, enrollment fees, computer fees, and others. Military tuition assistance is not the same thing as the GI Bill. The two benefits are separate and distinct. Military tuition assistance is not a loan that has to be repaid, either. It is one of the many benefits available to you during your service in the military.

The following represents the amount of military tuition assistance you can expect depending on which branch of the military you join:

Army	$250 per credit hour not to exceed $4,500 each year
Navy	$250 per credit hour with a limit of 16 credit hours per year
Air Force	$250 per credit hour not to exceed $4,500 each year
Marine Corp	$250 per credit hour not to exceed $4,500 each year
Coast Guard	$250 per credit hour not to exceed $4,500 each year

The process for applying to take advantage of military tuition assistance is different for each branch. You can check with your military education center for the necessary forms and procedures to get the ball rolling. Typically, your supervisor will have to sign off on any courses you want to take to make sure they won't interfere with the performance of your job. Thankfully, this benefit is rarely denied.

The GI Bill

If it seems like the educational benefits available to military personnel just keep on coming, it's not your imagination. There are few private organizations or scholarship programs that can come anywhere close to matching the incredible benefits available to military personnel. Perhaps one of the most well known of these benefits is the GI Bill. The GI Bill is an incredible benefit that can be used to pay for all of an undergraduate degree, a graduate degree, career training programs, licensing fees, and other educational pursuits. To qualify for full Post 9/11 GI Bill benefits, you must have a minimum of 36 months of active-duty service after September 11, 2001. Although the GI Bill provides a variety of benefits to service members, we'll stick to the educational benefits for our discussion.

The GI Bill (www.gibill.va.gov) was originally created in 1944 to provide educational and other benefits to the many thousands of service members who would soon be returning home from World War II. The original version of the GI Bill was a big success, enabling many veterans to earn a college degree, start a business, and buy a nice home in the suburbs. Many of the images we have from that era, such as the squeaky clean "Leave it to Beaver" household, would not have been possible without the GI Bill.

In 2008 the GI Bill received a major overhaul. The new version is popularly known as the Post 9/11 GI Bill. This new version beefed up the already-great benefits for those serving at least three years of active duty since September 11, 2001. The following is a summary of the major benefits of the new legislation:

- Funding for four years of tuition for an undergraduate college degree at an in-state public college or university

- The "Yellow Ribbon" program which provides additional funding for students who want to study at a participating private college or university
- Monthly living expenses for full-time students (Varies depending on location. This benefit is not available for students completing their degrees online.)
- An annual school supplies stipend of up to $1,000 (Covers books, miscellaneous fees, etc.)
- Unused benefits may be transferred to a spouse or children after serving 10 years

Although you must have 36 cumulative months of active-duty service to qualify for full Post 9/11 GI Bill benefits, you can still receive partial benefits if you need to access them early. But then again, with the availability of military tuition assistance, free challenge exams, and the ability to turn ACE evaluated military training into usable college credit, you may not need to. There's truly no shortage of great educational benefits available to military personnel.

Educational Benefits for the Reserves and National Guard

It's hard to argue that the educational benefits you can receive with an enlistment in any branch of the U.S. military are hard to beat. But what if you're interested in serving your country in uniform but don't want to do it full time? Maybe you've already got a great job you'd like to keep or have family obligations that would keep you from serving on a full-time basis. It's okay. You don't have to put your entire life on hold to serve. You can still join as a member of either the National Guard or in the reserves of any military branch.

As a member of the reserves or National Guard you will be required to go through a period of basic training and additional military career training. You will then be required to participate one weekend per month in activities at your assigned base in addition to participation in a continuous two-week training period once each year. And don't forget, as a member of the reserves or National Guard, you could always be called up for a full-time deployment at any time. After all, that's the whole purpose of having extra personnel on standby...just in case.

The benefits you'll receive while in the reserves or National Guard are very similar to those enjoyed by full-time military personnel. To start, if you qualify for certain military careers, you could be eligible for a signing bonus that's worth thousands of dollars. That alone should be enough to get most people's attention. You can also purchase low-cost health and life insurance and participate in the Federal Retirement Plan. And of course, the educational benefits are first-rate all the way.

If you join the reserves or National Guard, you can take advantage of free CLEP and DSST challenge exams. You will also qualify for military tuition assistance and can also qualify for the GI Bill (depending on your length of enlistment). You may even be able to qualify for a "kicker" which is a small stipend of a few hundred dollars each month you can use for living expenses. There are many people who join either the reserves or National Guard while full-time students and let their "part time jobs" pay for either part or all of their college degrees. As good as these benefits are, they get even better.

If you already have an existing student loan, by joining certain branches of the reserves or National Guard you may be able to have that loan completely paid down. This is a remarkable benefit. Let's see...rack up a student loan and then have the military take care of it? You betcha. You may be able to have anywhere from $40,000 to $50,000 of existing student loans paid for by qualifying for certain jobs and signing on for a six to eight year enlistment. Just a little something to think about. If you qualify for this incredible benefit, your student loan will not be paid down all at once; rather, a certain percentage of the loan will be paid down during each year of your enlistment.

Let's do a quick recap of the benefits you can receive with a part-time job with either the reserves or National Guard:

- You can get low-cost health and life insurance
- You can participate in the Federal Retirement Plan
- Certain military occupations qualify for a signing bonus
- You can take advantage of military tuition assistance
- You may qualify for the GI Bill (depending on length of enlistment)
- CLEP and DSST exams are free
- You may qualify for a monthly kicker to use for living expenses
- You may qualify to have an existing student loan paid down

This sounds a lot better than most part-time jobs I've heard of. And don't forget about the free military training you'll receive, too. Since you will be going through the same training programs the full-timers go through, you can earn college credit for your ACE evaluated military training by enrolling in a degree program with one of the Servicemembers Opportunity Colleges.

A part-time job with better than full-time benefits? The reserves and National Guard are that plus so much more.

Could one of these options be your ticket to a debt-free college degree?

ROTC for a Free College Degree

So far in this chapter we've taken a look at how you can earn a free college degree while serving in the military. We also took a good look at the free degree programs offered by the U.S. Service Academies in a previous chapter. But what if you're interested in earning a college degree before you enter military service and the U.S. Service Academies aren't exactly what you're looking for? Thankfully, you do have another option.

Through the Reserve Officers' Training Corps (ROTC) scholarship program you can attend college at any regionally accredited school in the United States that has an ROTC program and have your tuition paid for by the U.S. Government in exchange for a service commitment with either the U.S. Army, U.S. Navy, U.S. Marines, or U.S. Air Force (not available for the Coast Guard...sorry). Upon graduation you'll be commissioned as a junior officer in the military branch of the ROTC program you completed.

Technically, ROTC is a scholarship program that you must apply to and compete with others to be accepted. It's worth discussing, however, because it is very different from most traditional scholarship programs for one simple reason – the ROTC scholarship will pay for *all* of your degree program. To qualify for the full ROTC scholarship you can start applying during your senior year of high school. And if you already have some college behind you and would like to get in on the ROTC deal, you're not out of luck. Two and three-year scholarships are available that will pay for the remainder of your undergraduate degree. Acceptance into the program is based on a review of your grades and the results of an interview and a physical fitness test.

ROTC scholarships are designed to pay for all of your undergraduate degree. But that's not where the benefits end. If you are able to land one of these scholarships, you'll also qualify for additional money to pay for books and school fees. And to make the deal even sweeter, you'll also receive a monthly stipend to cover your living expenses that can go as high as $500 per month. This lets you focus like a laser on your studies instead of having to worry about taking on a part-time job to earn extra cash.

Need additional pay or benefits while working through the ROTC program? No problem. If you have received an ROTC scholarship, you can join either the reserves or National Guard for additional pay and benefits. Yes, you can do both at the same time.

If you are awarded an ROTC scholarship, you can expect additional military training while you work on your college degree. You will essentially be covering all of your basic training and additional officer training on a part-time basis while pursuing your degree full time. In addition to the courses you'll need for your degree program, you will also have to take electives courses in military science. Some schools, such as Virginia Tech, for example, award a minor in leadership for completing the 18 hours of military science courses in the ROTC program.

It's hard to argue with a free college degree, isn't it? But that's exactly what you'll get if you qualify for a ROTC scholarship. Why not consider this great option if you are looking for a way to fund your education and also like the idea of having a guaranteed job waiting for you after you graduate? Why not take the path that leaves you debt free?

Earn a Free Graduate Degree While Serving in the Military

The educational opportunities available to military personnel are not just limited to those at the undergraduate level. Did you know the U.S. government operates several graduate schools that are specifically for military personnel? You may have already heard of some of these. Just a few of them include the Air Force Institute of Technology, the Naval Postgraduate School, the Judge Advocate General's School of the Army (JAG), the National Defense University, and others. While many of these schools do charge tuition, free graduate degree programs are occasionally offered to military personnel. There is one specific military graduate school, however, where the tuition is always free. As long as you're accepted into any of this school's degree programs, tuition isn't an issue. There isn't any. This school is the Uniformed Services University of the Health Sciences. It's definitely worth a closer look.

The Uniformed Services University of the Health Sciences

The Uniformed Services University of the Health Sciences (USU) (www.usuhs.mil) was established in 1972 to train medical professionals in a variety of health sciences for all branches of the U.S. military. The school is located in Bethesda, Maryland, and only offers degree programs at the graduate level. There are three schools within USU totaling just over 800 students including the School of Medicine for training new physicians, the Graduate School of Nursing for advanced nursing training, and the Graduate School for the allied health professions. USU offers a variety of masters degree programs in addition to the Ph.D. in several fields and the Doctor of Medicine (MD).

In many ways USU is very similar to the U.S. Service Academies. In exchange for a free education, you are required to fulfill a service agreement after graduation. The length of the service agreement varies depending on which degree program you pursue. USU medical students, for example, are required to fulfill a commitment of seven years of active duty followed by six years in the reserves. As a USU student, you can choose to serve in either the U.S. Army, U.S. Navy, U.S. Air Force, or the U.S. Public Health Commissioned Corps.

One of the more interesting aspects of USU is that all students continue to receive full officer's pay and benefits while working full time on their degrees. Both nursing students and allied health students can keep their current rank and pay but the situation is a bit different for medical students. All USU medical students are ranked as junior officers (either second lieutenant or ensign). If you are a higher ranking officer, you will be temporarily demoted to a junior officer while completing your medical training.

Another very interesting aspect of USU is that its Doctor of Medicine program is open to both military personnel and civilians alike. You do not have to have prior military experience to be admitted. If you are admitted into this program as a civilian, however, you must join one branch of the U.S. military. You will immediately be ranked as a junior officer and receive officer's pay and benefits during your medical training. And of course, you will have a service commitment to fulfill immediately after graduation.

These days it's entirely normal for most medical students to take out significant six-figure student loans to get them through school. Not only is there a tuition-free alternative to such an expensive undertaking but it's also an option that pays you a full-time salary with benefits while you are working on your degree. It's hard to argue with a deal like that, isn't it?

If you are a medical specialist in any branch of the U.S. military or a civilian considering a career as a physician, you should definitely consider enrolling in a USU graduate degree program. Not only will a graduate degree allow you to take your career to the next level, but you'll be able to make it happen without taking out any student loans. You won't even have to use any of your GI bill benefits, either. You can save those benefits for later use. Or you could pass them on to your spouse or children if you have at least 10 years of service. With so many educational benefits available to military personnel, why not let the family in on it, too?

The Community College of the Air Force

Although we've almost come to the end of our look at the many educational benefits and opportunities available in today's modern military, we're still not finished. There's still one more great opportunity remaining for us to explore, the Community College of the Air Force (CCAF). And it's not a small opportunity either. It's literally huge. In fact, the CCAF is the largest community college system in the world.

Of all the U.S. military branches, the U.S. Air Force is the only branch to have its own two-year college that is dedicated to serving enlisted personnel. Through the CCAF (www.au.af.mil/au/ccaf/) those who are in the Air Force, Air National Guard, or Air Force Reserves can earn many different associate's degrees in the areas of aircraft and missile maintenance, allied health, electronics and telecommunications, logistics and resources, or public and support services. CCAF branch offices can be found at both military and civilian locations all around the world.

The CCAF is a unique institution in several ways. In addition to its size, the CCAF is also unique because it does not offer any courses of its own. Associate's degrees earned through the institution typically consist of a combination of both ACE evaluated military training and traditional college courses transferred in from other regionally accredited colleges and universities. The CCAF also accepts up to 30 credit hours of challenge exam credit toward the completion of a degree. And if you'll recall, CLEP and DSST exams are completely free for military personnel, making this a very affordable and fast route to an associate's degree. The CCAF has formed articulation agreements with dozens of colleges and universities to ensure that 100 percent of your CCAF associate's degree will be accepted and applied toward the completion of a bachelor's degree.

The CCAF does not charge any fees for the completion of any of its degree programs, although you will have to pay for any courses you take with other schools to use as transfer credit. You can minimize the number of courses you'll need to complete your degree program by taking full advantage of free challenge exam credits. In addition, you can pay for any additional courses you may need with either military tuition assistance or the GI Bill. By using these simple strategies, you can earn a CCAF associate's degree without spending any of your own money or having to worry about the burden of student loans. Your CCAF degree will truly be...a free college degree.

Although the CCAF is currently open only to members of the U.S. Air Force, Air Force Reserve, and Air National Guard, there is a movement underway to open it up to all military branches. If this does happen, perhaps the school will change its name to reflect its new mission (Community College of the Armed Forces?). This is one to watch!

Today's modern military is truly overflowing with opportunity, educational or otherwise. With the many different educational benefits available, you can truly go from zero college credits all the way to a bachelor's degree or higher without spending a dime of your own money or taking out any student loans. And you can do this while earning a living with your military job and gaining valuable experience for future employment at the same time.

Those who take the traditional college route often end up with a college degree and substantial student loan obligations. The military route, in comparison, leaves you with the same college degree, debt-free, and with valuable professional experience to put on your resume.

Opportunity. That's what today's modern military is all about. It's the closest thing to going to college for free and earning a full-time income at the same time that there is.

CHAPTER 12

Affordable College Courses
(Off the Discount Rack)

"Let every man, every corporation, and especially let every village, town, and city, every county and state, get out of debt and keep out of debt. It is the debtor that is ruined by hard times."

– Rutherford B. Hayes

Shopping around for a great deal…it's something people do every single day to make sure they get the lowest prices on the things they need, to protect themselves from being taken, and to hang onto as much of their hard-earned money as possible. Shopping around for the best prices is something we often take for granted in our lives. There are few people who would even consider purchasing a new television, computer, or car without first comparing prices for the best deals. And there are now many families that won't even consider shopping for groceries without bringing along a wheelbarrow full of coupons. Yet when it comes to higher education, the cost of a college degree is often a secondary consideration. Such an approach to selecting a school can be a recipe for financial disaster. The assumption is often made that getting into the "right" school is of utmost importance and that the student loans are something that can be taken care of later on in life after graduating and securing a high-paying job. It will just work itself out, right?

There are times when this strategy does indeed work but it's rare. If a student chooses her major well and is able to secure an upwardly mobile position with a solid company straight out of school, she may be able to pay down her student loans over the course of a number of years without making too many sacrifices. This is not always the case, though. Many recent college graduates who are new to the workforce are shocked at how small their paychecks are versus the size of their student loan payments. Sometimes there is so little left over after making the monthly student loan payments that they are forced to live lives of frugality out of necessity. There are some who even have to move back in with their parents just to make ends meet. While there's certainly nothing wrong with setting your goals on a great school with high academic standards, just be sure you know the costs up front and have mapped out a plan to earn your degree for as little money as possible prior to enrolling.

A key component of any debt-free degree plan is the ability to shop around for the best deals on tuition. Today, this is very easy to do since high-speed internet is common in most homes and there are now more schools offering courses online than ever before. There's no longer any need to drive from campus to campus to talk to admissions representatives just to gather information. Nor is there any need to even attend class. Thanks to the rapid growth of online courses, your search for the best deals on tuition can extend much further than your car can take you on a tank of gas. It can extend across the nation or even to another country, if need be.

The first place you should look for affordable college courses is, of course, your local community college. In most cases you simply can't beat the in-state tuition prices from the community college down the road. And since most community colleges now offer a large selection of online courses, you can earn quite a few credits without ever setting foot on campus or needing to adjust your busy schedule. The same holds true for upper-division courses. These days it's very common for both in-state colleges and universities to offer a large selection of courses and degree programs that can be completed either online, on the weekends, or during the evenings.

But what if your local school doesn't offer the courses you need? Or maybe you live in such a rural area that you don't even have a local school. Or perhaps you have a chaotic work schedule that makes taking traditional courses difficult (or impossible). And what if you're currently in the military or working for a company in a foreign country and you don't have access to a local college? While there are several factors that can stand in the way of taking traditional courses, this doesn't mean you have to completely put your pursuit of higher education on hold. Not at all. You just need to expand your search for a school that will meet your needs. You need to start looking on a national level for a few great sources of affordable college courses you can take from a distance, regardless of where you live or what your schedule looks like.

Since there are now literally thousands of schools that offer courses by distance study, how do you sort through them all to find the ones with the best deals without growing old in the process? You don't have to. I've done all the hard work for you. I've taken the time to sort through the high weeds to find several schools that offer great deals on distance study courses for college credit. You can take courses through any of these schools and then transfer them to the school you intend to graduate from. You don't even need to enroll in a degree program with *most* of these schools. You can take as many distance study courses as you need without matriculating in a degree program.

This is the part where we point fingers and name names (but in a really good way). These are the schools that have both great prices and a great deal of flexibility in course completion. The most logical strategy is to take as many courses as you can from the schools with the best prices and only use the more expensive schools for those hard-to-find courses.

Clovis Community College

Clovis Community College (www.clovis.edu) was established in 1961 in Clovis, New Mexico, and was named after the ancient Clovis people who lived in the area thousands of years ago. Clovis Community College has attracted a lot of attention in recent years for all the right reasons. Not only does the school offer outstanding academics, but it has also earned notoriety for its super-low tuition prices for out-of-state residents, which are easily among the lowest in the nation.

Clovis offers many different online courses through its eCampus program. The courses are semester based, so you will have clearly defined start and end dates for each course. Some Clovis courses require proctored exams while others don't. Those that don't simply calculate your grade based on the assignments you complete throughout the course. Figuring out which courses require proctored exams is very easy. The eCampus web site allows you to pull up the syllabus for each course and review it. If a proctored exam is required, it will be indicated on the syllabus.

Clovis's tuition is nothing short of remarkable. If you are a resident of New Mexico, you'll only pay $39 per credit hour. But if you're an out-of-state student, you can still get an incredible deal on tuition. Tuition for out-of-state students who are taking online courses is only $89 per credit hour. While that's certainly not a bad rate, it's not the end of the story. Clovis will let out-of-state students take up to six credit hours for the price of one three-credit hour course. That's $267 for two three-credit hours courses ($44.50 per credit hour). This unique offer is only valid for the summer semesters. The regular rate of $89 per credit hour applies for the spring and summer semesters. Clovis also has an option that lets out-of-state students take up to 18 credit hours for the price of 12 credit hours. This deal is available for all semesters, not just the summer. By taking advantage of this deal you can complete 18 credit hours for only $1,068 ($59 per credit hour).

Southeast Community College

Southeast Community College (www.southeast.edu) (SCC) is a large, multi-campus community college system in southeastern Nebraska. With its main campus located in Lincoln, the school also has two smaller campuses in Beatrice and Milford as well as 20 smaller off-campus sites serving many thousands of students in the region as well as online.

Southeast Community College has a couple of things going for it that make it worth mentioning. First, the school offers close to 200 online courses that are available each term (www.southeast.edu/online). In addition, the school also offers a variety of certificate and degree programs that can be completed entirely online. Four convenient terms are offered each year that start in January, March, July, and October.

One thing you should be aware of if you are considering taking SCC online courses is that the school uses the quarter system instead of the semester system. Thankfully, converting quarter hours to the more traditional semester hours is very easy. All you have to do is divide the number of quarter hours in a course by 1.5 to get the amount of semester hours the course is worth. For example, if you are taking a course that's worth 4.5 quarter hours, it will be worth three semester hours (4.5 / 1.5 = 3).

The second thing that makes SCC so interesting is its amazingly low tuition prices for out-of-state students. SCC only charges $54 per quarter hour for Nebraska residents, but the tuition for out-of-state students is, surprisingly, not that much more. If you are not a Nebraska resident and you want to take online courses through SCC, you will only pay $66.50 per quarter hour. SCC also charges a "student services fee," but at $1.25 per quarter hour it's hardly worth losing any sleep over. At these prices you could complete 30 credit hours (45 quarter hours) or one-fourth of a bachelor's degree for only $3,048.75.

Independent Study in Idaho

There's so much more to Idaho than watching potatoes grow. You can visit one of the state's many ski resorts, pan for gold, take a dip in the Lava Hot Springs, or if you are so inclined, you can sign up for one of the many independent study courses offered by the Independent Study in Idaho consortium (ISI) (**www.uiweb.uidaho.edu/isi**).

The ISI was created as a collaboration between four schools to pool their resources and offer a large assortment of independent study courses in both print and online formats. The four participating schools include the

University of Idaho, Idaho State University, Boise State University, and Lewis-Clark State College. These affordable independent study courses can be taken by anyone, regardless of where you live.

The ISI offers more than 100 independent study courses for college credit in more than 25 subjects. None of the courses are semester-based. You can enroll in any course at any time, regardless of course format. You will also have a generous amount of time to finish. You have one year from the time of enrollment to complete any course but you can always pay a $75 fee for an additional six-month extension, if needed.

When you enroll in any ISI course you will do so directly from the ISI web site. Each course is independently administered and college credit is awarded by one of the four member institutions. If you take several courses, you could easily end up with instructors from all four schools. Likewise, after you've completed all of the ISI courses you plan on taking, you will have to order transcripts from each ISI school you completed courses through.

There is very little difference between ISI's print-based courses and its online offerings. The primary difference is in how you access the study guide for each course. With the print format, you receive a printed copy of the study guide, while with the online version, you access it online. That's pretty much it. Many ISI courses also require proctored exams (but not all). Acceptable proctors include librarians, test center personnel, military education officers, and others.

All ISI courses have a very interesting feature that most schools simply don't offer. If you sign up for a course and for some reason it doesn't work out, you can switch to another course within the first 45 days without academic penalty. In other words, you get to "test drive" a course before making a commitment. If you do change courses, you will be required to pay a $25 fee plus $15 for any assignments already submitted. The original course end date will still be the same.

ISI courses are very reasonably priced at $100 per credit hour plus a $25 "administrative fee" for each course. This makes a three-credit-hour course only $325, regardless of where you live. At such a low price it would only cost $3,250 for 30 credit hours of coursework, or one-fourth of a bachelor's degree. I can live with that.

Louisiana State University

Louisiana State University (LSU) (**www.lsu.edu**), Louisiana's flagship state university, has been offering a world-class education to its parishes and beyond since 1860. What most people don't realize about LSU, however, is that it also offers many independent study courses for both high school and college credit at rock-bottom, closeout prices. If you are still in high school, you can certainly take advantage of LSU's high school courses if there's something interesting you want to take that your school doesn't offer, but for our discussion we'll stick with the college-level courses.

LSU offers nearly 200 independent study courses in more than 50 different subjects through its Independent and Distance Learning Department (**www.is.lsu.edu**). Both lower and upper-division courses are available. The majority of LSU independent study courses are offered in print format. After enrolling in a course, you receive a study guide that shows you what you need to do each step of the way toward course completion. Depending on the course, you will be writing papers, completing other assignments and/or taking proctored exams. Not all courses require proctored exams, though. Like Clovis courses, the requirement for proctored exams depends on which courses you take. Many LSU courses are also available in a "web enabled" format. This simply means you can access your study guide online and don't have to wait for it to arrive to get started. If you already have your course textbook, you can go ahead and dive into the course materials the same day you enroll.

There are no specific start dates for any LSU independent study courses, so you can enroll anytime of the year. Once enrolled in a course you have nine months to complete it, although it's possible to get an additional three-month extension for a $25 fee. And like Idaho's independent study courses, LSU also gives you the option to "test drive" a course and then switch to another one if, for some reason, you feel like it isn't working out. You can transfer to another course anytime within the first three months of your enrollment as long as no more than 50 percent of the course assignments have been submitted. You'll pay a $25 transfer fee to make it happen in addition to $10 for each assignment already submitted.

Although LSU does not offer any degree programs that can be completed by distance study, its distance learning department does offer four certificate programs. Three of these 15-credit-hour programs can be completed by anyone and do not require any prerequisites. These include certificates in liberal studies, business communications, and human services. Also offered is a certificate in accounting. This last certificate program is designed for those who have already completed a bachelor's degree in another field of study and are interested in switching careers and becoming accountants. Entry into the accounting certificate program requires the completion of a bachelor's degree in any subject and the completion of two semesters of intermediate accounting.

Okay, at this point you may be thinking LSU independent study courses sound pretty good. But how much do they cost? After all, this could be the big deal breaker, right? I've saved the best part for last. The tuition for any LSU independent study course comes in at only $105 per credit hour. LSU also tacks on additional fees totaling $88 per three credit hour course. This means a typical three credit hour course would only cost $403. That's only $4,030 for 30 credit hours, or one-fourth of a bachelor's degree. At these prices military tuition assistance would completely cover all of your annual tuition.

LSU's independent study courses are such a great deal that they could easily be a key component of nearly any college degree plan, regardless of which school you are attending. And since these courses are from a major state university, it's the educational equivalent of buying a high-end sports car for the price of a compact commuter.

The University of Arkansas

The list of major state universities offering independent study courses for college credit continues. Next up to bat is the University of Arkansas's School of Continuing Education and Academic Outreach (http://globalcampus.uark.edu).

If the independent study courses these schools offered didn't have the right stuff, do you think these big-name schools would even bother putting their names and weight behind them? Of course not. But they do, and for good reason. These courses are rigorous and challenging. They aren't "pie" courses you can work your way through in a couple of weeks. They require a great deal of dedication, perseverance, and self-motivation. Remember, you're completing the same assignments and taking the same exams the on-campus students are taking. You're just doing so from a different location (and you get to skip the boring lectures). The completion of any of these rigorous courses is fully deserving of college credit.

The University of Arkansas (UARK) is another university that has created an entire school to oversee its many distance study programs. Through the School of Continuing Education and Academic Outreach students can pursue a variety of undergraduate and graduate degree programs by distance study. The school even offers three doctoral degree programs that can be completed primarily by distance study with limited residency requirements. And for those who are looking for affordable independent study courses to use as transfer credit to another school, UARK does not disappoint.

UARK offers close to 100 independent study courses in nearly 20 different subjects in print format. Both lower and upper-level courses are offered. Some of these courses are now offered in a "web enabled" format, which gives you the option of submitting your assignments electronically. After enrolling in a course you have up to six months to complete it, although you can obtain a six-month extension by paying a $40 fee. UARK independent study courses also require proctored exams, so you'll need to secure a local proctor for this purpose.

Like several of the other schools previously mentioned, UARK also gives you the option to "test drive" a course and then switch to another one without academic penalty. You don't have much time to do so though, only 30 days, and the clock starts ticking the day you enroll in a course. If you do decide to transfer to another course, you will only be able to transfer 75% of your original course tuition less $7 for each assignment already submitted. You will also have to pay a $40 course transfer fee.

Tuition for any UARK independent study course is only $105.25 per credit hour in addition to $17 in additional fees per course. This means a typical three-credit-hour course is only $332.75, well below the national average. At this rate you can complete 30 credit hours or one-fourth of a bachelor's degree for only $3,327.50.

Mississippi State University

Mississippi State University (MSU) is the last major state university we're going to look at that offers independent study courses at affordable prices. The school offers a vast selection of more than 200 undergraduate independent study courses in both print and online formats through its Division of Academic Outreach and Continuing Education (**www.distance.msstate.edu**). Many of the courses offered are available in either format, so you can choose whichever is most convenient.

To be eligible to take any MSU independent study course, you must first be formally admitted into a MSU degree program. Although this requirement is different from most of the schools we've already covered in this chapter that let you take independent study courses without matriculating, don't let this stop you from considering MSU's affordable courses. There's no reason why you couldn't temporarily matriculate into a MSU degree program, take the independent study courses you need, and then transfer the credits you earned to another school. Incidentally, MSU offers a variety of degree programs that can be completed by distance study at both the undergraduate and graduate level.

MSU's online and independent study courses are very similar. The primary difference in the two course formats is in how you access your study guides. For online courses the study guides are accessed online, and for those taking independent study courses a printed study guide is used to guide you every step of the way. And, of course, you will have to secure a local proctor for any exams you need to take, regardless of course format. You can enroll in any MSU course at any time; there's no need to wait for a new semester to begin. Once enrolled in a course you have a maximum of one year to complete it, although you can purchase a three month extension for $50, if needed.

To enroll in your first MSU distance study course you must first submit a one-time admissions application with a $40 fee. Tuition for a three credit course is $449, or approximately $150 per credit hour. You could complete 30 credit hours, or one-fourth of a bachelor's degree, through MSU for only $4,490.

Brigham Young University

Brigham Young University (BYU) is quite possibly the king of independent study courses. Not only is it one of the largest religious-affiliated school in the United States, but it also offers over 200 independent study courses for college credit in addition to a generous selection of independent study high school courses. Both lower and upper-division college courses are available through BYU independent study in nearly 50 areas of study (http://ce.byu.edu/is/site). BYU offers so many independent study courses, you are almost sure to find what you need.

Most BYU independent study courses are available in both online and print formats. Like several of the other schools that offer independent study courses, the only real difference in the two formats is whether you access your study guide online or use a printed copy. There is no difference in assignment submissions or exams. All BYU independent study courses are open enrollment. You can enroll at any time of the year; there's no need to wait for a new semester to begin to get started. Once enrolled in a course you have one year to finish it although you can purchase a three-month extension by paying a $20 fee, if needed.

Most BYU courses require one or more proctored exams, but not all of them do. Some require only the completion of a certain number of assignments. You can easily determine which courses have proctored exams and which ones don't by reviewing the course descriptions prior to enrolling.

Have you ever received an assignment or an exam back with a grade that was, let's say, a little lower than you expected? Have you ever wished there was some way you could get a second chance to improve your score? A chance for a mulligan? Good news. Most BYU independent study courses give you that opportunity. For a fee of $10 per assignment, you can resubmit each assignment one time. And for a fee of $15 per exam, you can get a second shot at each exam to improve your score (one second attempt only). Assignment and exam resubmissions are available for most courses but not all.

Tuition for any BYU independent study course is $157 per credit hour. There are no extra fees for any courses but you will have to pay an extra $10 if you opt to receive a printed study guide instead of accessing the guide online. This makes a three-credit-hour online course only $471. Although this is more expensive than the courses offered by the other schools in this chapter, they are definitely worth keeping in mind due to the large number of independent study courses offered.

Liberty Academy/Liberty University

The last school we're going to take a look at is very different from the others. It doesn't offer any open-enrollment independent study courses and you do have to be enrolled in a program of study to take the courses it offers. So what's so special about it? Why bother mentioning it? Dual enrollment credit, that's why. This one is just for high school students.

Liberty University is the largest four-year university in Virginia and also one of the largest religious-affiliated schools in the United States. It has grown exponentially since its humble origins in 1971 as a small Bible college (originally known as Lynchburg Bible College) and there's no sign of it slowing down. In recent years Liberty has added an ABA-accredited law school and a new medical school is in development as well. The university is also known for the many high-quality online degree programs it offers at both the undergraduate and graduate level. This innovative school is doing everything right and it's exciting to imagine the new programs it will offer after a few more decades of growth.

In addition to its many academic programs at the college level, Liberty University also operates an accredited high school that offers students the opportunity to earn a high school diploma entirely online. The Liberty Online Academy (www.libertyonlineacademy.com) is a very popular option for many home school students all around the globe who are interested in graduating from an accredited school or who are looking for a structured curriculum (or both). Students can enroll in the Liberty Online Academy program at nearly any stage of their education, from early elementary school through high school.

Perhaps the most exciting aspect of Liberty Online Academy is its dual enrollment program. The school offers more than 30 online courses that award both high school and college credit at the same time. College credit is awarded through Liberty University and can be used as transfer credit to another school, or you can even complete an associate of arts degree through Liberty University as you finish your high school diploma. Just think about how remarkable it would be to graduate with both a high school diploma and an associate of arts degree at the same time without having to take any additional courses. Just think about how far ahead of your peers you would be. After graduating from high school you would only need two more years of college to finish a bachelor's degree. By the time your peers finish their first two years of college you could already have a bachelor's degree in hand and either be starting your career or going on to grad school.

The majority of Liberty Academy's online dual enrollment courses are offered in eight-week terms, although a few of the STEM (science, technology, engineering, and math) courses require 16 weeks to complete. In addition, all dual enrollment courses are priced the same as the high school's regular courses (non-dual enrollment) at $495 each. This is substantially less than what Liberty University charges for its college-level courses. Each dual enrollment course is worth .5 high school credits and three college credit hours.

If you're going to do any job, why not do it in the most efficient way possible—one and done? The same can be said for the lower-division courses that are required of most undergraduate degree programs. How many times do you really need to take an introductory psychology course before you've been sufficiently introduced to it? By taking dual enrollment courses in high school, the work you do gets to count twice, substantially decreasing the time it takes to complete a degree.

Shopping Around – It's No Longer Just for Appliances

We've come a long way in just a few short years. Instead of finding a great school and then figuring out how to pay for it, we can now shop around to compare tuition prices from around the country, even the world, and then take those courses from wherever we happen to be for college credit. Instead of visiting just a few local schools to check them out and get information, we can now go online to see if a particular school has what we're looking for, in both academics and price. Geography is no longer a limiting factor to obtaining a great education at an affordable price.

CHAPTER 13

Some Assembly Required

"Whenever you find yourself on the side of the majority, it is time to pause and reflect."

– Mark Twain

We've covered many different strategies in the preceding chapters that can be used to dramatically lower the cost of earning a college degree. Used individually, each strategy could easily result in thousands of dollars worth of savings. But what would happen if you were to combine several of these strategies in one degree plan? The results are nothing short of remarkable. Do you remember the bold assertion I made in the first chapter that it's possible to earn an accredited bachelor's degree for no more than $15,000? Well, the figure I gave you is a little on the high side. You can do it for less. Would you have believed me if I had quoted a lower price?

To be able to see how these strategies can dramatically lower the cost of earning a college degree, we're going to take a look at several examples of degree plans with some truly great schools. You should then be able to follow these examples to create your own degree plan and apply these strategies to nearly any school. It's now time to put it all together. But before we do, let's first do a quick recap of the debt-free strategies as a refresher.

- **Choose Your Major Well** (Ch. 1) – Be sure you are going into this with a solid career plan before jumping into a degree program. If you are thinking about earning a degree in a field that does not have a well-defined career path, you might want to reconsider.

- **Earn College Credit Through a Community College Before Transferring to a Four-Year School** (Ch. 2) – Take advantage of local community colleges for inexpensive in-state tuition. Most community colleges also offer a wide selection of online courses for those with scheduling conflicts.

- **Dual Enrollment Courses** (Ch. 2) – If you are still in high school, take as many dual enrollment courses as you possibly can. This allows you to earn both high school and college credit at the same time. These courses are usually heavily discounted from normal tuition prices.

- **Employee Education Benefits** (Ch. 2) – Many employers offer tuition reimbursements of up to $5,000 per year for employees to take college courses to improve job performance. This is money that does not have to be repaid and is considered an employee benefit the same as health insurance and vacation time.

- **Shop Around for the Best Tuition Deals** (Chs. 2 and 12) – Now that the internet is common in most homes, you can shop around for the best tuition deals and even take college courses by distance study, regardless of where the school is located.

- **Buy Used Textbooks Online** (Ch. 2) – Do an internet search for the ISBN number of your textbook and find the best deals online. After completing a course, list your book for sale with Amazon.com or another online company that lets you sell used books and recoup most of your initial investment.

- **Rent Textbooks Online** (Ch.2) – Take advantage of one of the many online textbook rental companies to rent your books instead of buying. You can rent for much less than purchasing new.

- **Consider Attending One of the Work Colleges** (Ch. 3) – The four work colleges (Berea College, Alice Lloyd College, College of the Ozarks, and Deep Springs College) do not charge any tuition. A free education is provided in exchange for working a part-time job either on campus or nearby.

- **Consider Attending a Tuition-Free School** (Ch. 4) – The three tuition-free schools (Macaulay Honors College, Curtis Institute of Music, and Webb Institute) do not charge any tuition. Graduates of these schools traditionally go on to lucrative and highly respected careers in their professions.

- **Consider Attending One of the U.S. Service Academies** (Ch. 5) – The five U.S. Service Academies (West Point, King's Point, Annapolis, The Air Force Academy, and The Coast Guard Academy) do not charge any tuition, room, or board. You will earn a degree from a highly respected school and are guaranteed a job immediately after graduation.

- **Use Challenge Exams to Earn Quick, Affordable College Credit** (Chs. 6 and 7) – Challenge exams are the fastest and most affordable way to earn college credit there is. Challenge exam credit is accepted by the overwhelming majority of schools in the U.S. Find out how many challenge exam credits your school will accept and then take as many as you can for your degree. Not only can you save many thousands of dollars with this strategy, but you can also reduce the time needed to graduate by one or more years. Challenge exams should be considered a high-priority strategy for any debt-free degree plan.

- **Use Portfolio Assessment to Turn Knowledge Obtained in a Nontraditional Way into College Credit** (Ch. 8) – Portfolio assessment is another widely accepted but little known strategy of turning knowledge acquired outside of the traditional college classroom into college credit. If you enjoy playing the guitar, for example, why not earn college credit in guitar performance and music appreciation by portfolio assessment?

- **Turn ACE Evaluated Job Training and Military Experience Into College Credit** (Ch. 8) – The little known strategy of turning ACE evaluated training into college credit is actually widely accepted by many schools all across the nation. You can use this strategy to turn on-the-job training, military training, and other training such as Straighterline courses into college credit that you can apply towards your college degree.

- **Consider Earning Your Degree Through One of the Assessment Schools** (Ch. 9) – The assessment schools (Charter Oak State College, Thomas Edison State College, and Excelsior College) accept many different sources of college credit, both traditional and nontraditional. The assessment schools are perfect for those who have a lot of credits from different sources and need a way of putting them together to earn a degree. These schools also make sense for many people just starting their higher education journeys since they are very affordable and accept a lot of challenge exam credit.

- **Turn Free FEMA Courses into College Credit** (Ch. 10) – FEMA offers many free courses that can be taken online that some schools accept for college credit.

- **Take Affordable ALEKS Courses Online for College Credit** (Ch. 10) – ALEKS offers several ACE evaluated courses that you can complete online and then turn into college credit. With an ALEKS course, you only need to work to an achievement level of 70 percent to complete the course.

- **Earn Free College Credit While Serving in the Military** (Ch. 11) – Many military training programs have been ACE evaluated for college credit. Some of these training programs, such as air traffic control, may be worth up to 60 credit hours! This alone is the equivalent of half of a bachelor's degree. If you are serving in the military, enroll in a degree program with one of the Servicemembers Opportunity Colleges (SOCs), take as many CLEP or DSST exams as the SOC will allow (free for active-duty personnel) and wrap up your debt-free degree by using military tuition assistance or the GI Bill.

- **ROTC for a Free College Degree** (Ch. 11) – There are many schools that offer ROTC programs that pay for your college degree and guarantee a job as an officer in the military upon graduation. ROTC also provides a small stipend to pay for living expenses while you are working on your degree.

- **Join the National Guard or Reserves for a Free College Degree** (Ch. 11) – If you prefer to keep your civilian life but still have a desire to serve your country, the National Guard or reserves lets you do so while qualifying for military tuition assistance and the GI Bill. You also qualify for free challenge exams and can turn your ACE evaluated military training into college credit by enrolling in a degree program with a Servicemembers Opportunity College.

- **Earn a Free Graduate Degree While Serving in the Military** (Ch. 11) – If you are in a healthcare-related career path, you can earn a free graduate degree through the Uniformed Services University of the Health Sciences while serving in the military where you can continue to receive full pay while working full-time on your graduate degree.

The Strategy

Before we get into specific examples of debt-free degree plans, let's take a brief look at *the strategy* that makes earning college degrees for such low prices possible. *The strategy* is really nothing more than a simple way of combining several different sources of affordable college credits to graduate for much less money than you would by earning all of your credits from one school. This is a strategy you can use with nearly any school, although it's best to stick with either in-state colleges and universities to take advantage of low in-state tuition, or with affordable online degree programs you've discovered from shopping around. *The strategy* is very simple and easy to understand.

The first thing you need to do is to look up the challenge exam policy for the school you intend to graduate from. We'll call this school your *target school*. How many challenge exam credits do they accept? Most schools will accept at least 30 credit hours of challenge exam credit while others will accept more. Because challenge exams are so inexpensive, they should form the foundation of your affordable degree plan. Don't forget that you can earn 30 credit hours of challenge exam credits for under $1,000. Earn as many challenge exam credits as your target school will allow.

If you are in the military or have completed some corporate training, you will also want to look up your target school's policy on ACE evaluated credit. Military personnel should always consider enrolling in a degree program with one of the many Servicemembers Opportunity Colleges to get maximum mileage from their military training.

After applying all of the challenge exam credits and/or ACE evaluated credits to your degree plan, you may need a few more credits to wrap up all of your lower-division degree requirements. This is where community colleges come in. You can complete the remainder of your lower-division degree requirements by taking affordable courses from your local community college or online from another community college with affordable tuition prices.

At this point you've completed half of a bachelor's degree for very little money. You now have two choices. First, you can transfer all of the credits you've earned directly to your target school and complete the remaining courses for your bachelor's degree from that school (typically around 60 to 68 credit hours). This is the ideal route to take if your target school offers a great deal on in-state tuition. If it doesn't, it's time to consider Plan B.

In the second option, all of your lower division credits are completed the same way. You then complete 30 credit hours of upper-division courses from one of the schools that offers affordable independent study courses (as outlined in Chapter 12) and then transfer all completed credits to your target school. You then take the remaining 30 to 38 credit hours of coursework from your target school to graduate. Most schools will let you transfer in up to 90 credit hours into a bachelor's degree program and then complete the remainder of your coursework through them to graduate. There is the occasional exception to this. Some schools may require you to complete the last 45 credit hours through them, although this is not typical.

If you follow this simple but highly effective strategy, you will be able to do something that seems so elusive to most people. You will be able to earn a college degree for very little money. You will be able to break free from the grip of the student loan monster and not have to be consumed with worry about making your next student loan payment or having to move in with family just to make ends meet. The importance of graduating debt-free cannot be understated. It represents opportunity, the opportunity to live a better life.

A Few Examples

Let's go ahead and take a look at a few examples of debt-free degree plans using *the strategy* with actual schools to get a good idea of how it all comes together. These degree plans can be implemented by anyone, regardless of where you live. The focus is on schools that offer online degree programs so that where you live will never be a limitation. Also, keep in mind that you don't have to rigidly follow these degree plans. They are merely examples of what is possible. Your own degree plan will be highly individualized, reflecting college courses already completed, ACE evaluated training already completed, and other factors. In other words, your degree plan must make sense for you.

The examples that follow only show CLEP challenge exams, Louisiana State University independent study courses, and community college credits from Clovis Community College. This was only done to keep things simple and so that you could make easy comparisons. You could easily substitute DSST or other challenge exams in place of CLEP. And for the independent study courses you could easily substitute courses from any school mentioned in Chapter 12 or courses from affordable in-state schools. Clovis Community College is used because their courses are so affordable. You could easily substitute courses from your local community college.

A Word on the Pell Grant

If you qualify for the Pell Grant, you will receive approximately $5,500 each year (the amount varies slightly from year to year) that you can apply toward your tuition until you complete a bachelor's degree as long as you are taking a full course load (at least 12 credit hours per semester). Any unused Pell Grant money is mailed to you in the form of a check from your school. You are free to spend this unused money any way you'd like. If you save leftover Pell Grant money from one year and then apply it to the next, in many cases it's possible to completely eliminate all of your tuition and other expenses. In many cases you can apply leftover Pell Grant money toward any fees, challenge exams, and any other degree-related expenses to graduate completely debt-free.

A Word on Military Benefits

All of the following degree plans can be completed at no out-of-pocket cost to you if you are on active duty in the military or in the reserves or National Guard. The costs are so low that all of your expenses can be covered by military tuition assistance, the GI Bill, and free challenge exams. All of the following schools are also Servicemembers Opportunity Colleges.

If you are currently in the military, the best strategy is to use all of the military tuition assistance available before tapping into your GI Bill benefits. You can then save your GI Bill benefits for grad school or something else.

Things Change

All of the information in the following examples is current as of the date of publication of this book (prices, policies on exam credits, and others). However, the one thing you can count on in the world of higher education is that things are always in a constant state of change. Schools may change their policies on the number of challenge exam credits they accept, the total number of credits needed to graduate, and so many other things. And of course, you can always count on tuition to go up, up, up. Rarely does it ever go down.

If you are interested in replicating one of the following degree plans and you discover that a particular school's policy or price on something I've quoted is different…guess what? It changed. Instead of focusing primarily on the prices I've quoted, I want you to focus more on the process. It is far more important that you have a solid understanding of *the strategy* so that you can design and implement your own degree plan through the school of your choice.

Associate's Degree Through Charter Oak State College

Charter Oak State College, one of Connecticut's state colleges and also one of the assessment schools, lets you earn either an associate's or bachelor's degree using a variety of nontraditional and traditional credits in many areas of study. The following is an example of an associate's degree through Charter Oak using a combination of ACE evaluated credits from Straighterline (which Charter Oak accepts as direct transfer) and CLEP exams. If you complete the majority of your degree requirements prior to enrolling with Charter Oak, you will only have to pay the College Semester Fee one time.

Charter Oak State College Application Fee	$75
Charter Oak State College Cornerstone Course	966
College Semester Fee (one semester only)	228
30 Credit Hours Through Straighterline	1,299
4 CLEP Exams Worth 6 Credit Hours Each ($77×4)	308
1 CLEP Exam Worth 3 Credit Hours	77
CLEP Transcript	20
Graduation Fee	205
Grand Total for Associate's Degree	$3,178

If you qualify for the Pell Grant, you can enroll with your local community college for one year to earn 30 credit hours in place of the Straighterline courses. Unless you are attending the most expensive community college in the nation, the Pell Grant will cover all of your community college tuition, leaving more than enough to cover the remainder of the degree requirements. This results in a totally free college degree.

Associate's Degree Through Thomas Edison State College

Thomas Edison State College is one of New Jersey's state colleges and also one of the three assessment schools that lets you earn a college degree using a variety of traditional and nontraditional sources of college credit. The following is an example of an associate's degree plan through Thomas Edison using affordable community college credits, CLEP exams, and free ACE evaluated FEMA courses (which Thomas Edison accepts as direct transfer). Although Thomas Edison does charge a substantial annual enrollment fee, you can avoid paying this fee more than once by completing the majority (or all) of the credits needed for your degree prior to enrolling.

TESC Application Fee	$75
Technology Services Fee	117
36 Credit Hours Through Clovis	2,136
6 Credit Hours from FEMA Courses (General Electives)	Free
2 CLEP Exams Worth 6 Credits Each ($77×2)	154
1 CLEP Exam Worth 3 Credits	77
CLEP Transcript	20
Annual Enrollment Fee	2,958
Capstone Course	663

Graduation Fee	280
Grand Total for Associate's Degree	$6,480

If you qualify for the Pell Grant, you would be able to use this benefit to completely pay for your community college courses. This leaves you with approximately $1,000 in out-of-pocket expenses to complete the degree.

Bachelor's Degree Through Thomas Edison State College

The following is an example of a bachelor's degree through Thomas Edison State College using CLEP exams, ACE evaluated Straighterline courses (which Thomas Edison accepts as direct transfer), ACE evaluated credits from either job or military training, and independent study courses. To make sure you only have to pay the annual enrollment fee one time, you can earn the majority of the credits required for your degree prior to matriculating.

TESC Application Fee	$75
Technology Services Fee	117
24 Credit Hours of Ace Evaluated Credit	Free
ACE Transcript	40
30 Credit Hours from Straighterline Courses	1,299
5 CLEP Exams Worth 3 Credit Hours Each ($77×5)	385
CLEP Transcript	20
48 Credit Hours Through Louisiana State University ($403×16)	6,448
Annual Enrollment Fee	2,958
3 Credit Capstone Course Through TESC	663

| Graduation Fee | 280 |
| Grand Total for Bachelor's Degree | $12,285 |

If you qualify for the Pell Grant, you can enroll with Louisiana State University and complete the 48 credit hours over a period of two years (12 credit hours per semester) and receive approximately $11,000 in Pell benefits. You can then apply any leftover grant money toward other expenses. Assuming you complete all lower-division requirements prior to enrolling with LSU, your total out-of-pocket expense for the degree is just over $1,000.

Bachelor's Degree Through Excelsior College

Excelsior College, a private, nonprofit school in Albany, New York, lets you use a wide variety of nontraditional and traditional sources of college credit to earn a college degree. Excelsior College is also one of the three assessment schools.

The following is an example of a bachelor's degree plan through Excelsior College using a combination of CLEP exams, ACE evaluated credits from job training or the military, and independent study courses. You can avoid paying Excelsior's annual student service fee of $485 by completing the majority of your credits prior to enrollment so that you can complete the degree in one year or less after matriculating.

Application for Admission	$80
Enrollment Fee	1,015
Annual Student Service Fee	485
4 CLEP Exams Worth 6 Credit Hours Each	308

($77×4)	
12 CLEP Exams Worth 3 Credit Hours Each ($77×12)	924
CLEP Transcript	20
48 Credit Hours Through LSU ($403×16)	6,448
9 Credit Hours of Ace Evaluated Credit	Free
ACE Transcript	40
3 Credit Capstone Course Through Excelsior College	1,170
1 Credit Information Literacy Course Through Excelsior	390
Graduation Fee	495
Grand Total for Bachelor's Degree	$11,375

If you qualify for the Pell Grant, you can enroll with LSU and complete 48 credit hours over two years (12 credit hours per semester). This will give you approximately $11,000 in Pell benefits you can apply to both your courses and other fees, leaving you with under $500 in out-of-pocket expenses to complete the degree.

Bachelor's Degree Through SUNY-Empire State College

Empire State College (www.esc.edu) is part of the State University of New York (SUNY) system, the largest university system in the United States. It offers many different affordable associate's, bachelor's, and master's degree programs that can be completed entirely online and has a very generous policy toward the acceptance of challenge exam credits, ACE evaluated credits, and credits earned through portfolio assessment. All lower-division course requirements for any Empire State bachelor's degree program can be completed using nontraditional sources of credit. Up to 96 credit hours can be transferred into a bachelor's degree program while the remaining 32 credits must be completed through Empire State (128 credits required to graduate).

Empire State College does not offer any majors (with the exception of its nursing degree program). Only concentrations are offered in 12 areas of study. Each student and a faculty adviser work together to create a highly individualized plan of study that will be followed to graduation. Empire State degree programs can be very traditional, if you prefer, and can include the same courses found in a traditional major. On the other hand, an individualized plan of study can give you great freedom to explore subjects of interest that you otherwise would not have been able to pursue in a traditional degree plan. You get to make the call.

Empire State's tuition for out-of-state students studying online is very affordable. You can take up to 16 credit hours per semester for only $246 per credit hour (including all additional fees), regardless of where you live. The following is an example of an Empire State College bachelor's degree using CLEP exams, independent study courses, and then finishing with Empire State online courses.

Empire State Orientation Fee	$50
4 CLEP Exams Worth 6 Credit Hours Each ($77×4)	308
1 CLEP Foreign Language Exam Worth 12 Credit Hours	77
8 CLEP Exams Worth 3 Credit Hours Each ($77×8)	616

CLEP Transcript	20
36 Credit Hours Through Louisiana State University ($403×12)	4,836
32 Credit Hours Through ESC ($246×32)	7,872
Empire State Term Fees ($135 per term for two terms)	270
Grand Total for Bachelor's Degree	$14,049

If you qualify for the Pell Grant, you will receive approximately $5,500 for each of the two years you are working on courses from LSU and Empire State. This leaves you with just over $3,000 in out-of-pocket expenses to complete the degree.

Bachelor's Degree Through Park University

Park University (www.park.edu) was established in Parkville, Missouri, in 1875 and was originally known as Park College. In the years that followed the school grew at an exponential rate and officially became Park University in 2000 to reflect its role as a comprehensive masters-level university. Park University is one of the top providers of higher education to military personnel and has 40 extended campus locations in states all across the nation, most of which are near military bases. Today, over 25,000 students are pursuing degree programs through the school either in person or online. Park is a very flexible school and offers a variety of associate's, bachelor's, and master's degree programs that can be completed entirely online.

Park University accepts up to 57 credit hours of challenge exam credit toward the completion of a bachelor's degree. The school is also a Servicemembers Opportunity College, accepting ACE evaluated military training for college credit. Park's tuition for active military personnel who are taking courses online is only $249 per credit hour. The tuition rate for civilians is $371 per credit hour. Also, some Park courses require an extra "course fee" of $20 to $50, but not all do. Since the course fees are hit and miss, we'll ignore them in the example.

The following is an example of a bachelor's degree through Park University using CLEP exams, ACE evaluated military training, Louisiana State University courses, and courses completed through Park University to graduate. This example is specifically for military personnel.

12 Credit Hours of ACE Evaluated Military Training	Free
ACE Transcript	$40
4 CLEP Exams Worth 6 Credit Hours Each ($77×4)	308
7 CLEP Exams Worth 3 Credit Hours Each ($77×7)	539
CLEP Transcript	20
33 Credit Hours Through Louisiana State University	4,433
30 Credit Hours Through Park University ($249×30)	7,470
Grand Total for Bachelor's Degree	$12,810

If you are on active duty in any branch of the U.S. military, you can use military tuition assistance to cover the majority of this program, with the exception of the 30 credits earned through Park University. Although military tuition assistance will not be enough to cover all of your tuition for that year, you can dip into your GI Bill to cover the remainder. This makes this degree program for military personnel…a completely free degree.

Bachelor's Degree Through Troy University

Troy University (www.troy.edu) was founded in 1887 in Troy, Alabama, and is one of the state's largest universities with nearly 30,000 students pursuing many different undergraduate and graduate degree programs. The school also offers a wide variety of undergraduate and graduate degree programs that can be completed entirely online (www.troy.edu/etroy). Troy is also a Servicemembers Opportunity College, accepting military training and other ACE evaluated training for college credit. In addition, the school accepts up to 60 credit hours of challenge exam credit which lets you quickly knock out the first two years of your degree through testing.

Troy's undergraduate tuition is slightly on the expensive side at $280 per credit hour, but is still manageable. The following is an example of a bachelor's degree through Troy using CLEP exams, military training, independent study courses, and then the remaining 30 credit hours through Troy to graduate.

Troy University Application Fee	$30
4 CLEP Exams for 6 Credit Hours Each ($77×4)	308
7 CLEP Exams for 3 Credit Hours Each ($77×7)	539
CLEP Transcript	20
15 Credit Hours of Military Training	Free
ACE Transcript	40
Servicemembers Opportunity College	50

Evaluation Fee	
30 Credit Hours Through Louisiana State University (403×10)	4,030
30 Credit Hours Through Troy University (30 x $280)	8,400
Graduation Fee	60
Grand total for Bachelor's Degree	$13,477

If you qualify for the Pell Grant, you will receive approximately $11,000 in grant money to complete the last two years of coursework for this degree plan. This leaves you with approximately $2,500 in out-of-pocket expenses to complete the degree.

Associate's Degree Through Liberty University

Liberty University (www.liberty.edu), one of Virginia's largest universities, offers many different degree programs at its Lynchburg campus in addition to a variety of associate's, bachelor's, and master's degrees that can be completed entirely online (www.luonline.com). The school is also a Servicemembers Opportunity College, accepting military and other ACE evaluated training for college credit. Liberty does not have any limit on the number of CLEP exams you can apply to a degree program. If you are working on an associate's degree through Liberty University, you only have to complete 15 credit hours through the school to graduate. The remaining 45 credits can be from challenge exams. If you are working on a bachelor's degree through Liberty University, you can complete (almost) all of your lower-division courses by challenge exam (with the exception of a couple of lower-division courses in religion).

Although Liberty's tuition is a little on the high side at $304 per credit hour (full-time student rate), the ability to use challenge exams to complete many of your degree requirements makes the school worth discussing. The following is an example of an associate's degree through Liberty University using CLEP exams and Liberty's online courses.

Liberty University Application Fee	$50
Technology Fee ($175 Per Term)	175
4 CLEP Exams for 6 Credit Hours Each ($77×4)	308
7 CLEP Exams for 3 Credit Hours Each ($77×7)	539
15 Credit Hours Through Liberty ($304×15)	4,560
Graduation Fee	100
Grand Total for Associate's Degree	$5,732

The Pell Grant is a little tricky with this one since you will only be a full-time student for one semester. Any Pell Grant funds you qualify for are not distributed all at once. Rather, half of the funds are distributed in the fall semester of a typical school year while the remainder are disbursed in the spring semester. If you do qualify for the Pell Grant, you will only receive funding for one semester, or half of the full grant of $5,500 ($2,750). This leaves approximately $3,000 in out-of-pocket expenses to complete the degree.

Bachelor's Degree Through Liberty University

The following is an example of a bachelor's degree through Liberty University using CLEP exams, military or other ACE evaluated training, independent study courses, and Liberty's online courses. The example assumes you are working on your degree full time to qualify for Liberty's full-time student rate of $304 per credit hour (regardless of where you live).

Liberty University Application Fee	$50
Technology Fee ($175 Per Term)	175
3 CLEP Exams for 6 Credit Hours Each ($77×3)	231
4 CLEP Exams for 3 Credit Hours Each ($77×4)	308
24 Credit Hours of Ace Evaluated Training	Free
Ace Transcript	40
36 Credit Hours Through Louisiana State University	4,836
30 Credit Hours Through Liberty ($304×30)	9,120
Graduation Fee	100
Grand Total for Bachelor's Degree	$14,860

If you qualify for the Pell Grant, you will receive approximately $11,000 for the two years of course work. This leaves you with only $4,000 in out-of-pocket expenses to complete the degree.

Bachelor's Degree Through Peru State College

Peru State College (**www.peru.edu**) is one of Nebraska's three state colleges and is also the oldest institution of higher learning in the state. The school was established in 1865 in the small town of Peru, immediately following the U.S. Civil War. Peru State College is located on a beautiful, tree-filled campus and is often referred to as the "Campus of a Thousand Oaks." Peru State is also a Servicemembers Opportunity College, accepting ACE evaluated military training for college credit. Military personnel can take Peru State courses right on the Offutt Air Force Base in nearby Sarpy County, or they can pursue a variety of degree programs entirely online.

Peru State is a very attractive option to many for several reasons. First, the school's affordable tuition is hard to ignore. The rate for online courses is only $210 per credit hour, regardless of where you live. In addition, Peru State doesn't nickel and dime you to death with extra fees like so many schools do these days. The only extra fees you can expect are a matriculation fee and a graduation fee, and these are so low they're hardly worth mentioning. Peru State is also very generous in accepting challenge exam credit, letting you compete all of your lower-division course requirements with this method.

The following is an example of a bachelor's degree through Peru State using CLEP exams, ACE evaluated military training, and online courses taken through Peru State to graduate.

Peru State College Application	Free
Matriculation Fee	10
4 CLEP Exams for 6 Credit Hours Each ($77×4)	308
7 CLEP Exams for 3 Credit Hours Each ($77×7)	539
CLEP Transcript	20
15 Credit Hours of ACE Evaluated Training	Free
ACE Transcript	40
60 Credit Hours Through PSC (60 x $210)	12,600
Graduation Fee	<u>30</u>

Grand Total for Bachelor's Degree	$13,547

If you qualify for the Pell Grant, you will receive approximately $11,000 in grant money for the two years of course work. This will reduce your total out-of-pocket expense to complete the degree to approximately $2,500.

Associate's Degree Through Fort Hays State University

Fort Hays State University (**www.fhsu.edu**), located in Hays, Kansas, was founded in 1902 and is Kansas's fourth largest state university. Fort Hays State University accepts up to 30 credit hours of CLEP exam credits toward an undergraduate degree and is also a Servicemembers Opportunity College, accepting ACE evaluated military training for college credit.

Fort Hays offers a variety of degree programs that can be completed entirely online at both the undergraduate and graduate level. The school's tuition for undergraduate courses is a remarkable $178.30 per credit hour for any online student, regardless of where you live.

The following is an example of an associate's degree through Fort Hays using CLEP exams and online courses. The degree can be completed in one year.

Fort Hays Admission Fee	$30
6 CLEP Exams for 3 Credit Hours Each ($77×6)	462
2 CLEP Exams for 6 Credit Hours Each ($77×2)	154
CLEP Transcript	20

30 Credit Hours Through Fort Hays ($178.30×30)	5,349
Grand Total for Associate's Degree	$6,015

If you qualify for the Pell Grant, you will receive approximately $5,500 in grant money for one year. This will reduce your total out-of-pocket expense to complete the degree to approximately $500.

Bachelor's Degree Through Fort Hays State University

The following is an example of a bachelor's degree through Fort Hays using a combination of CLEP exams, Clovis Community College courses (or your local community college), and Fort Hays courses. Fort Hays requires a minimum of 124 credit hours to graduate with a bachelor's degree.

Fort Hays Admission Fee	$30
8 CLEP Exams for 3 Credit Hours Each ($77×8)	616
36 Credit Hours Through Clovis Community College	2,136
64 Credit Hours Through Fort Hays ($178.30×64)	11,411.20
Grand Total for Bachelor's Degree	$14,193.20

If you qualify for the Pell Grant, you will receive approximately $5,500 for each of the three years it will take you to complete the coursework, or $16,500 ($5,500×3). Although you will have to pay for the CLEP exams up front, there will be enough leftover Pell Grant funds to reimburse you for this expense. This results in – a free college degree.

Bachelor's Degree Through Columbia College

Columbia College (www.ccis.edu) is a private liberal arts college in Columbia, Missouri, that was founded in 1851 and has nearly 14,000 students. There is no connection to the similarly named Columbia University in New York City. The two schools are completely separate and distinct.

Columbia College is noteworthy for several reasons. First, the school accepts up to 60 credit hours of challenge exam credit, half of a bachelor's degree. Columbia is also a Servicemembers Opportunity College, accepting ACE evaluated military training for college credit. In addition to its many degree programs offered on campus, the school also offers a variety of online degree programs at both the undergraduate and graduate level. Columbia has very few fees to worry about and its online tuition is an agreeable $240 per credit hour, regardless of where you live.

The following is an example of a bachelor's degree through Columbia College that combines ACE evaluated military training, CLEP exams, independent study courses, and courses taken through Columbia to graduate.

Columbia College Application Fee	$35
30 Credit Hours Of ACE Evaluated Military Training	Free
ACE Transcript	40
2 CLEP Exams for 6 Credit Hours Each ($77×2)	154
6 CLEP Exams for 3 Credit Hours Each ($77×6)	462

CLEP Transcript	20
30 Credit Hours From Louisiana State University	4,836
30 Credit Hours From Columbia College ($240×30)	7,200
Graduation Fee	75
Grand Total for Bachelor's Degree	$12,822

If you qualify for the Pell Grant, you will receive approximately $11,000 for the two years you'll need to complete the coursework. This leaves approximately $2,000 in out-of-pocket expenses you'll need to complete the degree.

When most people think about reducing the cost of higher education, they usually think about academic or sports scholarships. This is the common thought process. But you're not like most people, right? Just by reading through a book on the many strategies available that let you earn a college degree for very little money, I already know something about you. I know you are someone who is not afraid to think outside of that narrowly-defined box that most people live in. You're not afraid to expand your horizons and look for a different path to accomplish your goals, a path that will lead you to a kind of freedom that is completely foreign to most people. The freedom we're talking about is financial freedom, the ability to earn a college degree with little or no debt.

As the last words in this final chapter are being written, the story of a recent college graduate is making the news. This young woman racked up nearly $200,000 in student loans for her bachelor's degree and the average starting salary for her major is about $35,000 per year. Needless to say, she is drowning in debt. Even after moving back in with her parents and working full time, she can barely keep up with her student loan payments. To give herself at least a glimmer of a promising future, she is trying to get the word out about her situation through various news organizations and has set up a website to accept donations to pay down her student loans.

You don't have to make the same mistake this young woman did. You don't have to be crushed under the weight of a mountain of student loan debt that may take decades to repay. You are now armed with the necessary knowledge to map out a college degree plan before you even begin your academic journey. Your college degree will last a lifetime; monthly payments on a student loan shouldn't last anywhere near as long. The path down the road less traveled is now well lit. Take it and you can live a life that is free from the shackles of student loan debt.

CHAPTER 14

Looking Back

"Hindsight is always 20/20."

– Author unknown

By now you may be wondering what path I chose to complete my college degree and if there's anything I would do differently if given the chance to do it all over again. Truth is, I didn't complete just one degree. I finished three of them and graduated debt free each time. I completed a BS in liberal studies with a concentration in sociology from the University of the State of New York, Regents College (now known as Excelsior College) in 1997. I then took a three-year hiatus from school before entering grad school and completing an MBA from Regis University in 2002. After that, I worked as an accountant for several years before deciding to return to the college scene once more to earn an accounting degree to give me the credential I needed to advance in my career. In 2009 I graduated with a BS in accounting from Peru State College.

The strategy I used to earn a degree through Excelsior College was very simple. I took affordable community college courses from a nearby school and then transferred the credits to Excelsior. I then shopped around for the best deals I could find on upper-level courses to complete the degree. Since I had a demanding full-time job while I was working on my first BS, independent study and online courses allowed me to complete all upper-level coursework and exams on my own schedule instead of someone else's. The puzzle pieces fit perfectly. And because I was able to shop around for the best deals, I was able to pay for the degree out-of-pocket as I went.

The strategy I used to earn the MBA was also very simple. Since I had a full-time day job, I knew the program would have to be online. If I had gone with a local school to complete the degree I would have had to quit my job to do so, since none of them offered evening or weekend programs. Quitting my job simply wasn't an option. I shopped around for online MBA programs from reputable schools that had the best prices on tuition and the lowest fees. After starting my search it didn't take long to discover Regis University in Denver, Colorado. The school had a very strong reputation, very high rankings, and very affordable tuition.[4] Not only that, but I could complete the entire degree online. Perfect. Due to the low tuition, I was able to pay for the degree out-of-pocket as I went.

When it came time to start my search for a good school for earning an accounting degree, I once again sought out a program that could be completed entirely online from a school with a strong reputation. For those who work full time, online programs really are the best way to go. I found many great options but ultimately decided to go with Peru

---

[4] Regis University's tuition has increased substantially (more than doubled) since I was a student there. There are still many great schools that have affordable grad school tuition that are just waiting to be discovered by shopping around. Never give up searching for a great deal.

State College in Peru, Nebraska. The school was Nebraska's oldest college and its tuition was unbelievably low, even for out-of-state students.

By the time I matriculated with Peru State College I had discovered the power of using challenge exams to quickly test out of lower-division courses. I was able to take a few CLEP and DSST exams, complete 30 credit hours through Peru State, and then transfer in the rest to graduate. It took two years to finish the BS in accounting, mainly because I was only able to take two courses at a time since I worked full time. The entire degree only cost about $5,000 and I paid for it out-of-pocket as I went.

Would I do anything differently if I had to do it all over again? Sure, you bet. For starters, I would have taken as many challenge exams as my degree program would allow up front. This alone could have knocked off one or two years of coursework, resulting in substantial savings as well as being able to graduate in less time. When I first started my higher education journey, I simply didn't know enough about these incredible exams to take advantage of them. Thankfully, I was able to incorporate them into my second bachelor's degree.

The military option is also something that I would have given much more thought to if I had known about the incredible benefits earlier. As a lifelong aviation enthusiast, the U.S. Air Force, Air Force Reserve, or Air National Guard would have been the most likely contenders. I would have either gone to a school that had Air Force ROTC or enlisted in the Air Force, reserves, or National Guard, and used the military benefits to complete a degree while serving at the same time. Either way I would have graduated debt free. Either option would have been a winner.

Lastly, I discovered that one of the work colleges, Alice Lloyd College, was less than a two-hour drive from where I lived after I had already completed my first bachelor's degree. I had certainly heard of the school before because of its close proximity but I was completely unaware that the school did not charge any tuition. It was something that no one bothered to mention. Either that or no one around me knew (probably the latter). If I had known about the incredible opportunity this school offered, I certainly would have applied.

The book you are now finishing is the book I wish I had when I was starting my own higher education journey. In many ways this is a book I wrote to myself, as if it was somehow possible for an older (and wiser) me to address a much younger (and less-informed) me. Even though I would have done a few things differently if I had the necessary information earlier in life, I don't regret the path I chose one bit. I was still able to graduate completely debt-free and besides, I'm now able to pass along the information I discovered to you in a comprehensive guide that gives you every piece of information you need to map out your own debt-free degree plan. You can now take advantage of the information and strategies I discovered to earn your degree for much less money and in less time than what most people believe to be possible.

www.ingramcontent.com/pod-product-compliance
Lightning Source LLC
LaVergne TN
LVHW051828080426
835512LV00018B/2771